CONTENTS

TABLES

FIGURES

PREFACE

The concept of *open regionalism* has deep roots in the experience and discussion of economic growth and trade expansion in the Asia-Pacific region. It has more recently entered the mainstream debate about the future of the world trading system as two ASEAN states prepare to host major meetings in 1996: the APEC Leaders' meeting in Manila in November; and the inaugural ministerial meeting of the World Trade Organization in Singapore in December.

This book presents an introduction to the idea of *open regionalism*. It brings together nine papers that have been presented to conferences in recent years in Singapore, Indonesia, Malaysia, Australia and the United States. A number of these papers have been published elsewhere in various international journals and books and a few are published here for the first time. They are brought into this one volume to provide convenient access to one author's contribution to the evolution of one important dimension of *open regionalism* — its application to trade liberalization.

Three chapters (Three, Four and Five) provide a taste of the development of *open regionalism* as an operational concept in the debates leading to Asia-Pacific Economic Co-operation's (APEC's) commitment at Bogor in November 1994 to free and open trade by 2010 (developed countries) or 2020 (newly industrialized and developing economies). In several of these debates, colleagues in ASEAN thrust upon me the responsibility of providing an alternative vision of APEC regionalism, based on *open regionalism*, to that being expounded at the time by some in North America.

Chapter One outlines the concept *open regionalism*, and makes a few introductory remarks about its origins.

Chapter Two defines *open regionalism* and suggests a rationale for it in economics and political economy. Chapter Two was first presented at a joint meeting of the American Economics Association and American Council of Asian Economic Studies in Anaheim, California, in January 1993. This paper is reproduced with the permission of the *Journal of Asian Economics*.

Chapter Three explains that "closed" or discriminatory approaches to regional free trade — the conventional "free trade area" — are not feasible in the Asia-Pacific, at least at this time in history. This chapter was first presented to a meeting of the Pacific Economic Co-operation Council in Kuala Lumpur in March 1994. Chapter Four outlines an approach to regional trade liberalization based on an old strand of thought about *open regionalism* in the Asia-Pacific. This chapter was first presented at a seminar on Asia-Pacific Economic Co-operation at the Institute of Southeast Asian Studies in Singapore in June 1994. Chapter Five was presented at a conference organized by the Centre for Strategic and International Studies in Jakarta literally on the eve of the Bogor Summit. It foreshadows the APEC Leaders' commitment to free trade, and explains that such a commitment could be implemented in practice only within a framework of *open regionalism*. The original paper, like Chapter Three, was first presented within a two person debate with Fred Bergsten, then Chairman of APEC's Eminent Persons Group, that came to focus on the relative merits of open and discriminatory regionalism. Chapter Five is reproduced with the permission of the Centre for Strategic and International Studies in Indonesia.

Chapter Six was first presented to the World Trade Congress in Singapore in April 1996, preparatory to the inaugural Ministerial Meeting of the World Trade Organization in November. It is

reproduced with the permission of the Singapore Trade and Development Board.

Chapter Seven was first presented at the International Monetary Conference in Sydney in June 1996.

Chapters Eight and Nine reach back to earlier times and provide some historical perspective. Eight, with my colleague Peter Drysdale, was presented in the early stages of the United States renewal of interest in discriminatory free trade, at a conference at the Institute for International Economics in Washington D.C. in September 1988. It is reproduced with permission of Peter Drysdale and the Institute of International Economics.

Chapter Nine was first presented at a meeting of the Victorian Economic Society in Melbourne in August 1980. It argues that Western Pacific trade expansion can be promoted by regional negotiations to reduce trade barriers on a most-favoured-nation basis. It was amongst the background papers at the inaugural Pacific Economic Co-operation Council (then the Pacific Community Seminar) meeting at the Australian National University in Canberra in September 1980. Some echo of this discussion is seen in Professor Sir John Crawford's influential summing up of discussion at that historic event (Crawford and Seow 1981).

All chapters are as originally presented, with a few abridgements and corrections of infelicities in expression.

The papers form part of the larger research contributions of economists based at the Australian National University, and of the wider community of economists interested in Asia-Pacific Economic Co-operation on both sides of the Pacific Ocean.

I have been working with Peter Drysdale at the Australian National University on Asia-Pacific economic co-operation since the late 1960s. Peter's energy and faith was the fuel of much of the scholarly as well as official interest in organized forms of Asia-Pacific economic co-operation, in the two decades before the formation of APEC in November 1989 brought it to centre stage in the international affairs of our region. Other important intellectual interaction in the developments of my own thoughts on these matters were with Sir John Crawford, Nancy Viviani and Heinz Arndt from the early days, and Stuart Harris, Andrew Elek, Hal Hill, Christopher Findlay, David Vines, Kym Anderson, Peter Lloyd and Richard Snape over the past decade or two, all in Australia. Amongst overseas colleagues, my thoughts on these matters have developed in interaction over long periods with, amongst others, Hugh Patrick, Larry Krause, Jagdish Bhagwati, Saburo Okita, Kiyoshi Kojima, Ippei Yamazawa, Narongchai Akrasanee, Mohamed Ariff, Noordin Sopie, Hadi Soesastro, Mari Pangestu, Frank Holmes, Jesus Estanislao, Soogil Young, Victor Fung, Chia Siow Yue and Lee Tsao Yuan. When Fred Bergsten entered the discussion from the late 1980s, his different view based on contemporary United States political economy, was helpful in sharpening the argument. Helen Hughes was always a sceptic at home base about all regional co-operation, keeping all of us on our toes.

All of us, and others with whom we have laboured in these fields, have been seeking to make sense of the growth of production and trade that has been flourishing in East Asia and the Pacific over several decades. The reality guided the ideas that explained them, *open regionalism* amongst them. And the ideas can make some contribution to shaping the reality that continues to unfold.

Observation of the practice of international economic policy in ASEAN was always an important inspiration of the intellectual developments reflected in this book. ASEAN has now moved into a central role in giving the concepts operational form, with the APEC Leaders' meeting in Manila in November 1996, and the first ministerial meeting of the World Trade Organization in December the same year.

I am grateful for the contact that I have had with the Institute of Southeast Asian Studies which has provided a major forum for research and publication on foreign economic policy and relations in Southeast Asia and the wider Asia-Pacific region over the past quarter century.

I am grateful as well for the assistance that I have received in preparation of the manuscript from Hilda Heidemanns, Maree Tait, Carol Kavanagh, Iain Rowe, Sonya Bodger and Carolyn Sweeney.

Canberra
June 1996

1
OPEN REGIONALISM
Reality Shapes an Idea

Open regionalism was the term that defined APEC's aspirations in the early ministerial meetings in Canberra (1989) and Seoul (1991), and set the scene for the first Leaders' summit in Seattle (1993) and the commitment to free and open trade and investment in Bogor (1994).

It has been described pejoratively as the *mantra* of Asia-Pacific Economic Co-operation, and as an "oxymoron", embodying contradictory concepts of open-ness and regionalism.

There is some sense in which it has been a *mantra*, in the early stages of bringing the diverse economies of the Asia-Pacific together in APEC. And *open regionalism* is, indeed, an oxymoron if the term *regionalism* is confined by its most prominent historical usage — in relation to discriminatory free trade areas and customs unions in the style of the North American Free Trade Area and the European Union.

But in the Asia-Pacific, *open regionalism* has a precise meaning: regional economic integration without discrimination against outsiders. This is the concept that emerged over two decades of discussion of economic co-operation in the Asia-Pacific from 1969. When I defined the term in this way at Anaheim in January 1993, participants in the American Economic Association/American Council of Asian Economic Studies joint meeting were struck neither by its novelty, nor with any sense that this was controversial (Chapter Two).

While there were attempts from supporters of traditional forms of discriminatory regionalism in the Pacific to blur or broaden the meaning of *open regionalism* (Eminent Persons Group 1993), the precise meaning has mostly survived. In the precise form (although with some anxiety about the sometime blurred edges), the term and the concept have in 1996 entered discussion of the international trading system. Note the strategic role ascribed to it in Singapore in April 1996 by the inaugural Director-General of the World Trade Organization, Renato Ruggiero (1996):

I see the ensuring that national barriers are not just replaced by regional ones, but that, on the contrary, regionalism and multilateralism converge at the end of the road as the main challenge facing the multilateral system at present, one which will shape its future and help shape the world of the 21st century.

The trading system is now moving forward on two tracks — regional and multilateral. Regional trade initiatives are expanding and have ambitions to expand further. It would be wrong to assume that the multilateral system is in a period of dormancy.... Where we are perhaps lacking, however, is in showing a level of ambition at least equivalent to that of the major regional systems. Let me explain what I mean.

Some recent regional initiatives are truly gigantic, at least in perspective; take for instance the European project to create a preferential trade area with all the Mediterranean countries by 2010; or the framework agreement between the EU and MERCOSUR or the plan set out in the Miami Declaration to create a free trade area of the Americas by 2005; or, finally, APEC's commitment to create a free trade area in two stages between 2010 and 2020.

The multilateral system has no comparable road map towards the elimination of all trade barriers. However, some of the newer regional groups (such as APEC and MERCOSUR) contain a commitment which is very important for the future of the multilateral system: this is *open regionalism*.

Of course, we need to be clear about what *open regionalism* means. Among the different possibilities, I see two basic alternatives.

The first is based on the assumption that any preferential area under consideration will be consistent with the legal requirements of the multilateral system. This would mean that such areas could at the same time be legally compatible with the WTO's rules and preferential in their nature, which means they would be an exception to the m.f.n. clause which is the basic principle of the multilateral system. The possibility of making such a legal exception to the m.f.n. principle within the rules was conceived in a completely different time and situation. Today, with the proliferation of regional groupings, the exception could become the rule, and this would risk changing completely the nature of the system.

The second interpretation of *open regionalism* is the one I hear from a number of governments who are members of APEC or MERCOSUR. In this scenario, the gradual elimination of internal barriers to trade within a regional grouping will be implemented at more or less the same rate and on the same timetable as the lowering of barriers towards non-members. This would mean that regional liberalization would be generally consistent not only with the rules of the WTO but also — and this is very important — with the m.f.n. principle.

The choice between these alternatives is a critical one; they point to very different outcomes. In the first case, the point at which we would arrive in no more than 20 to 25 years would be a division of the trading world into two or three intercontinental preferential areas, each with its own rules and with free trade inside the area, but with external barriers still existing among the blocs. Is this the sort of world any of us would want?

I leave you to imagine the consequences of this vision in terms of economic and political equilibrium; the problem of those who did not fit into any of the blocs would be a serious one — and where would China and Russia be in such a world?

The second alternative, on the other hand, points towards the gradual convergence on the basis of shared rules and principles of all the major regional groups. Each one of the existing and emerging regional groupings has to contribute with vision and determination to ensure that at the end of the process both regional and multilateral approaches will have contributed to full liberalization in a free global market. At the end, we would have one global free market with rules and disciplines internationally agreed and applied to all, with the capacity to invoke the respect of the rights and obligations to which all had freely subscribed. In such a world there could and must be a place for China, Russia and all the other candidates to the WTO. The global value of a system based on rules and disciplines will be a limited one as long as some major players remain outside.

Ruggiero's statement to the 1996 World Trade Congress in Singapore lays out the issues precisely. The recent proliferation of regional arrangements has the potential to marginalize the multilateral rules and disciplines which alone can provide the means for effective management of the issues that arise from the globalization of production. The concept of *open regionalism* can, in principle, reconcile the proliferation of regional arrangements with the multilateral system. But only if *open regionalism* is applied in its original Asia-Pacific usage, with all participants in regional trade liberalization processes adhering to the most favoured nation rule.

After Ruggiero's April 1996 statement, Dr Jesus Estanislao, leading Philippines economic analyst and policy adviser, outlined a strategy for ASEAN leadership of the international system into freer multilateral trade based on *open regionalism*.

Estanislao, addressing the Asia-Pacific Profiles conference in Hong Kong in May 1996, suggested that ASEAN members should offer to multilateralize their commitments to internal free trade within the ASEAN Free Trade Area (AFTA) by 2003. This is broadly consistent with ASEAN countries' practice to date in implementing AFTA trade liberalization. The new element would be the commitment to continue the practice in future. If agreed by ASEAN economic ministers, it could be presented to the Manila APEC meetings in November as a joint approach to the requirement for countries to present individual action plans related to the implementation of the Bogor free trade commitment. This could be expected to encourage substantial responses from APEC partners. If the responses were forthcoming, APEC, in support of the ASEAN initiative, would be in a strong position to lead the December WTO meeting into support for eventual multilateralization of other major regional free trade arrangements, including the European Union. This would lay the basis for a new WTO objective of eventual global free trade.

The practical opportunity was underlined by the Vice President and Commissioner for Trade, Leon Brittain, in Australia in June 1996, when he noted that the European Union would not fail to respond commensurately if APEC did in fact move towards free trade on a multilateral basis on the Bogor timetable (2010 and 2020).

There is a large step between opportunity and its realization. It may be that too few APEC and WTO members, or too few sufficiently influential members, yet comprehend the potential for moving towards global free trade through utilization of the potential of *open regionalism*. In that case, we could expect much less from the APEC Summit in November and the WTO Ministerial Meeting in December than would otherwise be available. However, movement in the directions proposed by Estanislao, short of firm commitment, would still be helpful to progress in Manila and Singapore towards multilateral free trade.

Regionalism without Trade Discrimination

What is the point of a regional arrangement if it does not discriminate in favour of members over non-members? If there is no favouring of members over non-members, what is to be gained above each country pressing on with unilateral liberalization?

The papers in this book develop answers to these questions.

The term *open regionalism* has been given descriptive as well as analytic content.

In its early usage, *open regionalism* was mainly descriptive of the reality of Asia-Pacific trade expansion as it emerged in the post-war decades. The huge expansion of trade and investment, the deepening integration amongst Asia-Pacific economies was driven by market forces once individual governments had gone a certain distance in liberalizing external trade and payments. Regional intergovernmental agreements and institutions and formal trade discrimination made little contribution or none.

The discussion of Asia-Pacific economic co-operation from the late 1970s recognized this reality. It sought to strengthen and to extend the reality, at first through efforts to improve private sector knowledge of opportunities within the region, and then to render the conduct of economic policy within individual economies more sensitive to its effects on Asia-Pacific neighbours (Drysdale and Patrick 1979; Soesastro 1983). This was a main thrust of the Pacific Community Seminar at the Australian National University in Canberra in September 1980 (Crawford and Seow 1981). The introduction to the Pacific Community Seminar's proceedings by the Chairman Professor Sir John Crawford, contains the first published use of the term *open regionalism* in English, attributing it to "some Japanese views".

This strand of thinking about *open regionalism* — co-operation across national borders in a region to reduce transactions costs — became a distinctive feature of discussion of Asia-Pacific economic co-operation. Governments could augment private processes by providing some public goods to reduce the costs of international exchange. The role of governments in support of open regional trade expansion in the Asia-Pacific came to be known as *trade facilitation* (PECC 1992; APEC 1992; Elek 1992*a*, 1992*b*, 1992*c*; Eminent Persons Group 1993, 1994).

Trade facilitation is an important means whereby regional co-operation can provide benefits to participants, without any steps being taken to exclude outsiders from the benefits. In the nature of things, some *trade facilitation* measures will confer benefits on outsiders, and others will not.

Alongside *trade facilitation*, trade liberalization on a non-discriminatory basis has represented a second dimension of *open regionalism* in the Asia-Pacific. Three separate elements can be identified. One is regional co-operation in multilateral and other extra-regional trade negotiations to secure non-discriminatory trade liberalization at home and abroad. The second is co-operation to promote non-discriminatory liberalization in a number of regional economies, to strengthen political support for and economic gains from liberalization in each one of them. This element came to be known as *concerted unilateral liberalization* in the lead-up to and at the Osaka meeting of APEC leaders in 1995. The third is agreement to secure non-discriminatory liberalization of trade in sectors in which export expansion deriving from the liberalization is concentrated within the region.

The first element of regional trade liberalization on a non-discriminatory basis, regional co-operation in multilateral and other fora to secure trade liberalization abroad and at home, was an early focus of ASEAN economic co-operation, and was incorporated into the Asia-Pacific discussion from ASEAN sources (Garnaut 1980, Garnaut and Anderson 1980). There was early progress in practical regional co-operation amongst Western Pacific economies in multilateral negotiations in the lead-up to what became the Uruguay Round, and within APEC in the settlement of the Uruguay Round (APEC 1992, 1993; Bergsten 1994; Eminent Persons Group 1994). Estanislao's statement to Asia-Pacific Profiles 1996 is an important development within this strong tradition. Chapters Two, Three, Five, Six, Seven and Eight contribute to this tradition of *open regionalism*.

The second element of regional trade liberalization on a non-discriminatory basis, concerted non-discriminatory liberalization, has entered the discussion of *open regionalism* in the Asia-Pacific through recognition of the dynamics of trade liberalization and trade expansion in the Western Pacific since the mid-1980s. Over this period, all Western Pacific member economies of APEC, except possibly Papua New Guinea, have embarked upon far-reaching trade liberalization. The fact that many have followed this course at the same time has supported the process in each — by expanding the gains of each economy's own liberalization, through demonstration of the domestic gains of unilateral liberalization, and by weakening common political arguments against unilateral liberalization ("why give away bargaining coin"; or "others are defending themselves so we should do the same"). *Concerted unilateralism* was accepted at the Osaka Summit in 1995 as a principal mechanism through which Asia-Pacific economies would achieve free and open trade in the region by 2010 or 2020. Its rationale is discussed in Chapters Two, Three, Five and Eight.

Discussion of the third element, non-discriminatory liberalization in sectors in which regional suppliers are likely to contribute a major part of associated export expansion, grew from recognition that some polities may be reluctant to support trade liberalization if major export expansion were enjoyed by economies that had not reciprocated. The motive for aversion to free-riding might be *schadenfreude* (Chapter Four), or, especially in large economies, reluctance to give away bargaining coin. It was recognized at an early date in the Asia-Pacific discussion of regional trade liberalization that the concentration of high trade barriers in sectors in which regional suppliers dominated exports to the region, allowed the region, to a considerable extent, to have its cake and eat it too. Sectors in which regional suppliers were dominant exporters could be selected for liberalization (Chapter Nine, and its reflection in Crawford and Seow 1981, p.3; Chapter Four; Drysdale 1988). Alternatively, the concentration of high trade barriers in sectors in which regional suppliers were dominant exporters to regional markets could be relied upon to produce a similar effect even with general trade liberalization (Chapter Eight, Chapter Four). Sectoral liberalization on a most-favoured-nation basis was part of the APEC discussion in the preparation for the Manila leaders' meeting in 1996.

Why Non-Discrimination?

Why has the discussion of Asia-Pacific regional trade liberalization been concerned to avoid discrimination? There are three types of reasons. The first is highly practical, and in the Asia-Pacific has been compelling. If a region is committed to working within the rules of the GATT and WTO, a discriminatory free trade area must, for good reason, meet a number of demanding conditions. It must establish substantially free trade over a specified period (now held to be ten years). It must define a schedule and a timetable for achievement of substantially free trade. None of these conditions have been thought to be practically attainable for free trade within the Asia-Pacific since APEC was established in 1989 — not in the

United States, not in China, not in ASEAN, and not in Japan. If regional trade liberalization were to be secured through a conventional free trade area, progress would have to await an indefinite time while divisive negotiations explored the possibility of meeting the GATT-WTO conditions.

The second is that the crucial trading interests of Asia-Pacific economies extend outside APEC — to Europe, to other developing and transitional economies, notably in Indochina and South Asia, and to neighbouring Russia. A conventional free trade area would introduce unwelcome tensions into trade relations with these economies, and deter internationally-oriented reform and growth in the developing and transitional economies.

The third comes out of straightforward economic analysis. Trade discrimination introduces unnecessary costs of trade diversion. This has probably been important to ASEAN economies choosing so far to implement their commitments to trade liberalization within the ASEAN Free Trade Area (AFTA) mostly on a most-favoured-nation basis. It also played a supportive role in the general reduction of external trade barriers in Australia and New Zealand as internal barriers were reduced in line with the Closer Economic Relations agreement.

For all three of these reasons, trade liberalization without discrimination — *open regionalism* — has played a central part in the discussion of Asia-Pacific economic co-operation since the early days.

The proceedings of the first Pacific Community conference contain clear reference to all of the cautionary points that later caused the Asia-Pacific to steer clear of a traditional free trade area. The cautions came particularly from ASEAN participants, but the Chairman's summary records general support for the idea that "EEC-style" (note that then there was no NAFTA) "discriminatory trading arrangements were inappropriate in the Pacific" (p.29); "that arrangements should be outward-looking" (p.29); and "the need to avoid unnecessarily bureaucratic structures" (p.30) (Crawford and Seow 1981).

Successive meetings of the Pacific Economic Co-operation Council and its task forces began to use the term *open regionalism* more frequently, culminating in a major statement in 1992 (PECC 1992). The strongest PECC focus was on trade facilitation, which was given increasing substantive content over time, and which has remained a central feature of Asia-Pacific Economic Co-operation.

The shape of Asia-Pacific co-operation in trade liberalization was influenced consistently by Japanese, ASEAN and later Chinese commitment to non-discriminatory arrangements within the multilateral system and resistance to highly formalized negotiations and binding agreements within complex institutions.

Throughout the evolution of thought on Asia-Pacific economic co-operation, ASEAN was important for its articulation of constraints on institutional development, and as a model — the latter particularly in relation to regional co-operation to achieve liberalization within the multilateral trading system. Australian Prime Minister Bob Hawke led off with precisely this point in a speech (Hawke 1983) in Bangkok in November 1983, calling for Western Pacific co-operation in shaping the agenda of a new round of multilateral trade negotiations. Note also the emphasis on *open regionalism* — regional trade liberalization without discrimination — in this precursor to a series of consultations amongst senior trade officials in the Western Pacific, an antecedent of APEC:

> Co-ordinated action by the ASEAN countries is a contemporary and successful example of regional action contributing to improvements in the multilateral trading system ...
>
> Australia for its part would strongly support a new round of multilateral trade negotiations, but only if it was confident that it would address seriously and effectively these matters of special

importance to Australia, New Zealand and our developing country neighbours in the Asia-Pacific region.

The chances of achieving an appropriately structured round of negotiations would be greatly enhanced if the countries of this region were to apply their full and united weight to its achievement.

But if our best efforts should fail to overcome the consistent commitment of many of the old industrial countries to patterns of trade that discriminated against Australia, the ASEAN countries, and other countries in our region, we should not let that be the end of the matter.

There would still be scope for negotiations on trade expansion among countries within our own region, on a non-discriminatory basis, but focused on commodities in which countries in our own region are the most competitive suppliers.

Progress on the "Western Pacific" agenda within the Uruguay Round satisfied demands for *open regionalism* for a number of years, during which its content was expanded and elaborated by the Pacific Economic Co-operation Council (PECC). PECC was strongly influenced by ASEAN perspectives and cautions about a formal discriminatory regional area. These cautions were again to the fore in the sculpting of Prime Minister Hawke's call (1989*a*) for the establishment of an Asia-Pacific inter-governmental institution that became APEC, in Seoul in February 1989:

> ... I must stress that my support for a more formal vehicle for regional co-operation must not be interpreted as suggesting by code words the creation of a regional trading bloc.... Australia's support for non-discriminatory multilateral trading solutions in the GATT framework is clear, long-standing and unambiguous.

ASEAN ministers at the Brunei Post-Ministerial Conference in 1989 made explicit the conditions of ASEAN participation in APEC, and these were reflected in Prime Minister Hawke's opening statement (Hawke 1989*b*) at APEC I in Canberra in November 1989:

> Some of the earlier thinking about Asia-Pacific co-operation was confused by a mistaken belief that we could or should move towards some kind of Pacific trading bloc.
>
> Then, as now, such an idea was an impractical one that failed to take into account the diversity of the region's economic development.
>
> More seriously still, such an outcome would be a foolish one, in that it would run counter to the region's absolutely compelling interest in the maintenance of a strong and open multilateral trading system. It is on such a system that the region's economic prosperity has been built and continues to rely.

These sentiments were reflected in the APEC I Chairman's summary (Evans 1989):

> We are all agreed that an open multilateral trading system has been, and remains, critical to rapid regional growth. None of us support the creation of a trading bloc.

This approach was reinforced in the subsequent confirmation of continued participation in APEC by ASEAN economic and foreign ministers in Kuching in 1990. The *Kuching Consensus* specified that:

> APEC should not be directed towards the formation of an inward looking economic or trading bloc, but, instead, it should strengthen the open, multilateral economic and trading systems in the world.

Liberalization within the multilateral system and avoidance of a Pacific trading bloc, alongside regional *trade facilitation*, were entrenched at the Seoul APEC meeting in 1991, and in contemporaneous commentaries by officials closely associated with the early APEC meetings (Elek 1992*e*):

> APEC's guiding principles, built on the intellectual foundations laid by the Pacific Economic Co-operation Council (PECC) since 1980, stipulate that co-operation should be outward-looking, building consensus on a gradually broader range of economic issues. Participation is to be open-ended.... Regional trade liberalization is to be promoted, provided it is consistent with GATT principles and not to the detriment of other economies.

Ambitions for APEC trade liberalization expanded in the lead-up to the first Leaders' Meeting in Seattle in 1993. The APEC Eminent Persons Group (EPG) recommended "that APEC members agree now to (1) adopt an ultimate goal of free trade in the region and (2) determine in 1996 the timetable and strategy for reaching the goal" (EPG 1993). APEC Leaders in their Economic Vision Statement from Seattle "welcomed (d) the challenge .... to achieve free trade in the Asia-Pacific". They did not, however, accept the challenge, partly due to the reluctance of some to sign up to "free trade in the region" without knowing more about the shape it would take.

The second report of the EPG (1994) emphasized the *trade facilitation* dimension of *open regionalism*. On trade liberalization, however, it departed from the longstanding traditions of Asia-Pacific economic co-operation, with recommendations that would have introduced an element of discrimination into regional trade relations, requiring (to meet the over-riding commitment to consistency with GATT rules and principles) approval under Article 24 of GATT. Other statements in the second EPG report led in another direction, seeming to be consistent with the established traditions of APEC *open regionalism*. The departure from the established interpretation of *open regionalism* generated debate, within the EPG and without.

The second APEC Leaders' Meeting in Bogor accepted the EPG's recommendation on free and open trade within the region. The meeting's language on trade liberalization in some ways favoured non-discriminatory trade liberalization, but was open to alternative interpretations. Malaysian Prime Minister Mahathir sought to make the commitment to non-discrimination explicit in an addendum to the Bogor Declaration, the status of which was itself contested. The uncertainty of interpretation was compounded when Australian Prime Minister Paul Keating explicitly referred to the possibility that the Bogor Declaration's commitment to free trade might be implemented under Article 24 of GATT, and therefore allowing discrimination, in a comment in the Australian Parliament (Keating 1994).

Clarity came at the 1995 Leaders' Meeting in Osaka. The path to free trade was defined consistently with traditional conceptions of *open regionalism*, that is, through non-discriminatory liberalization. The APEC Leaders emphasized the role of *concerted unilateral liberalization*. The scene had been set for the concept that had emerged from the long conversation about Asian Pacific economic co-operation, to play a larger international role in the APEC and WTO meetings hosted by ASEAN members in late 1996 (Ruggiero 1996).

2
OPEN REGIONALISM
Its Analytic Basis and Relevance to the International System

I Introduction

Open regionalism involves regional economic integration without discrimination against economies outside the region.

Open regionalism can be contrasted with "discriminatory regionalism", of which the Customs Union, the Free Trade Area and the Preferential Trading Area are three alternative forms, and the European Community (EC) and North American Free Trade Area (NAFTA), the contemporary models. With discriminatory regionalism, official trade barriers at members' borders are lower for trade with members than with non-members.

Economic ideas are shaped by, and in turn help to shape, economic reality. The early post-war discussion of, and movement towards, the establishment of the European Economic Community inspired, and was influenced by, the sophisticated theory of customs

This paper was first presented at a joint meeting of the American Economics Association and the American Council of Asian Economic Studies, Anaheim, California, January 1993. Reproduced with permission of the *Journal of Asian Economics*.

16

unions that was developed through the 1950s and early 1960s (Lipsey 1960; Vanek 1965).

The concept *open regionalism* has emerged from and has helped to shape the practice of economic co-operation in the Asia-Pacific region. The concept and the term were descriptive of an emerging reality of regional economic integration in the Asia-Pacific region in the 1970s. *Open regionalism* was articulated by the first Pacific Economic Co-operation Conference (PECC) in Canberra in 1980, and by the first Asia-Pacific Economic Co-operation (APEC) Ministerial Meeting in Canberra in 1989, as an ideal for the future development of economic relations in the Asia-Pacific region. The concept has been elaborated and its essential elements defined more precisely over time, including within PECC (1992) and APEC (1992).

Whilst *open regionalism* has emerged from the discussion and reality of economic co-operation in the Asia-Pacific region, it has wider application. In a world in which economic regionalism has renewed legitimacy, it is, potentially, the alternative to the disintegration of the multilateral trading system into exclusive discriminatory blocs.

This paper seeks to define *open regionalism* analytically. Section II relates *open regionalism* to earlier discussion in the literature of "market" and "discriminatory" integration. Section III discusses the role of resistances to trade flows to economic integration in a general framework, within which "market" and "discriminatory" integration are special cases. Section V examines the special case of official trade discrimination. (Sections IV to VI draw from Garnaut 1991*b*).

The discussion in Sections II to IV (these sections rely heavily on Drysdale and Garnaut 1993) leads to the identification in Section V of three analytic elements of *open regionalism*: "open" policies in relation to official barriers to trade (protection); the role of regional co-operation in reducing non-official barriers to trade;

and regional integration through market processes, independent of government. These three elements are respectively the focus of the following three sections. Section VI looks at the relationship of official barriers to trade at countries' borders, that is, protection, to *open regionalism*. It contrasts the traditional post-war approach to trade negotiations amongst advanced industrial economies, in which each country regards a reduction in its own border protection as a "concession", to the pattern of trade liberalization that has emerged in the Western Pacific region, in which unilateral liberalization has been widely adopted for the benefits that it generates in the home country. This part of the paper notes that whereas the traditional approach leads to the conceptualization of the trade negotiations "game" as a "prisoners' dilemma", the Western Pacific pattern has evolved into what has been called a "prisoners' delight". Section VII analyses the contribution to *open regionalism* of government intervention other than protection, through the regional provision of public goods. Section VIII looks at the reduction of trade barriers that are not related to the roles of government, through market pressures. Section IX brings the discussion back to the Asia-Pacific origins of *open regionalism*. A concluding section draws out some implications for United States trade policy and the international system.

II Market and Discriminatory Integration

The concept of *open regionalism*, and its relationship to "institutional" or "discriminatory" regionalism, owe something to older discussion of economic integration.

Cooper (1974) was one of the first to draw attention to the various origins of regional trade expansion with his identification of "market integration" around institutional and legal barriers to trade, involving capital movements and other forms of economic interchange.

The concept of "market integration" was recognized through the 1970s as being descriptive of rapidly expanding economic relations within the Asia-Pacific region (Crawford and Seow 1981).

By contrast, economic integration in Europe has flourished within the institutional arrangements of the European Community. European integration discriminates against economies outside the region: the removal of barriers to trade has been accompanied by the maintenance of some external barriers, while others, such as those affecting agricultural trade, have become a greater encumbrance to global trade growth.

The terms "market integration" and "institutional integration" have been useful in drawing attention to the difference between European and Asia-Pacific economic integration. But they are misleading to the extent that they are interpreted literally. The emergence of new institutions to reduce the costs of international trade expansion, to a considerable extent private but increasingly inter-governmental, has been important to Asia-Pacific trade expansion. And the important role of integrative institutions, embodying large elements of official discrimination in Europe and now North America, does not exclude market pressures from a major role in intra-regional trade expansion (Milner 1991, p.7).

Following Drysdale and Garnaut (1993), this paper retains Cooper's term "market integration" for the case where the initiative has remained primarily with enterprises acting separately from state decisions, and where official encouragement of regional integration does not include major elements of trade discrimination. The term "discriminatory" is preferred to "institutional" integration for arrangements of the European Community and NAFTA kind. *Open regionalism* includes "market integration" and also integration that is facilitated by government policy to the extent that this does not involve discrimination against outsiders.

III Trade Resistances and Economic Integration

"Economic integration" can be defined as movement towards one price throughout the global economy, for a unit of merchandise, a service or a factor of production (Drysdale and Garnaut 1993). The normal state of world markets is one of considerable **disintegration**: wide price disparities exist, between regions of the world, between countries and between regions within countries.

Disintegration persists because of barriers, or resistances, to trade. Resistances to trade are defined as phenomena which prevent or retard the movement of commodities in response to price differentials.

One line of literature that has developed out of analysis of Asia-Pacific experience distinguishes two basic types of resistances: **objective** resistances, and **subjective** resistances (Garnaut 1972; Drysdale and Garnaut 1982).

Objective resistances can be overcome by firms only at some objectively determined minimum cost. They comprise principally transport and other (including physical communications) costs of overcoming distance, and official barriers to trade (principally protection).

Subjective resistances comprise a range of social, psychological and institutional factors which cause prices to vary across geographic space by larger margins than can be explained by the necessary costs of overcoming **objective** resistances. **Subjective** resistances derive from perceptions of risk and uncertainty about property rights and valuations at various stages of trade transactions, from imperfection in the information available to firms, and from the processes through which firms take decisions that affect the volume, geographic direction or commodity composition of trade.

Johnson (1968) suggests a slightly different categorization of the same phenomena, distinguishing "geographic distance and the transport cost of overcoming it", "differences of political and legal systems, culture and language that differentiate nations from one another as market areas" and "protection". Drysdale and Garnaut (1982) judge that it is more useful analytically to see the "differences of political and legal systems, culture and language" as factors affecting the costs of overcoming subjective resistances to trade, rather than as separate resistances in themselves.

Resistances are present in all economic transactions, whether domestic or international. They are commonly, although far from universally, lower within than between countries. This difference is one of the factors distinguishing international from inter-regional trade. There are, however, important exceptions to the common pattern. Regional price disparities within some large, weakly integrated economies (say, Indonesia and China) can exceed disparities, at least for many commodities, between major cities exposed to trade between countries (Arndt and Sundrum 1975). Border trade occurs between adjacent regions of two countries with a common border when the cost of overcoming intra-national resistances exceeds the cost of overcoming international resistances.

The costs of overcoming various resistances vary across bilateral trading relationships. The divergences from the law of one price associated with resistances to international trade are typically very large. Amongst **objective** resistances, while official barriers have received most consideration in public discussion and the literature, today these are less important than transport costs in relation to imports of most manufactured goods into advanced industrial economies. There are exceptions, of which textiles and clothing import restrictions into the OECD are the most important. (Agricultural trade in Europe, North America and Northeast Asia is obviously a separate case, where border protection remains very important.)

Subjective resistances can be larger than **objective** resistances (Garnaut 1972). Sung (1992) underlines the importance of these considerations in his discussion of the huge and expanding role that Hong Kong is playing in China's trade — a role that contributes much of Hong Kong's rationale today. Interestingly, Hong Kong's role in the China trade has expanded as China has opened to the outside world, despite reductions in resistances to direct trade between established enterprises in China and in the rest of the world (Sung 1992). This paradox is resolved upon examination of the effect of China's internationalization in increasing the range of firms and commodities participating in foreign trade, and therefore the transaction costs in dealing with them.

The costs of overcoming various types of resistance to bilateral trade, **objective** and **subjective**, are closely inter-related. Economies of scale affect the cost of overcoming all except official resistances; **objective** transport and communications costs up to quite large levels of bilateral trade; and **subjective** resistances of all kinds. There are externalities in one firm's investment to reduce the cost of overcoming resistances to trade: investment in the organization of a new pattern of transport or communication reduces costs for other firms in the bilateral trading relationship; and investment in information to support a new pattern of trade provides information to others — including through observation of the resulting trade expansion itself.

These two characteristics of the costs of overcoming resistances to trade together introduce conservative bias and stability into bilateral trade patterns. They increase the time lags in the adjustment of trade patterns to new relative cost relationships, which in any case are long, as enterprises search for and process information, and respond to it. They cause trade expansion associated with reduction in one type of resistance to trade, to reduce the cost of overcoming all other resistances. And they demonstrate the importance of institutions, both private and public, from the internally integrated multinational enterprise to mechanisms to enforce contracts in international trade, in determining the costs of overcoming resistances to trade.

IV Resistances, Trade Creation and Trade Diversion

The cost of overcoming trade resistances in general has not been treated systematically in the theory of international trade. **Subjective** resistances make a cameo appearance in the theory of the product cycle (Vernon 1966), but disappear without influencing the whole corpus of theory.

The exception is the theory of protection (Corden 1971, 1974) and customs unions (Lipsey 1960; Vanek 1965), which analyse the impact of official barriers to trade that are, respectively, uniform and differentiated across countries. Insights from the theory of protection and customs unions are of considerable value in understanding the impact of resistances more generally on trade and welfare.

"Multilateral" reductions in official resistances to a country's international trade unambiguously expand the welfare of the country itself, and the rest of the world. However, reductions in official resistances in some bilateral relationships but not in others may raise or lower the welfare of countries involved in the resulting bilateral trade expansion, depending on the balance of trade creation and trade diversion. (When we use the concepts in this way, from the theory of customs unions, we will sometimes refer to classical trade creation and classical trade diversion.) Such differentiated reductions in resistances in some bilateral trading relationships unambiguously reduce trade with and the welfare of countries in the rest of the world, outside the trade-expanding bilateral relationships, unless the income-increasing effects of trade creation are very large compared with other economic effects.

Reductions in non-official resistances to trade are in some ways similar to and in some ways different from reduction in official barriers.

A reduction in non-official resistances to trade, derived from private firms' investment in information about opportunities in a new bilateral trading relationship, or in building business relationships to support a new pattern of bilateral trade, will typically be differentiated across bilateral trading relationships. There may be a shift in some trade from established bilateral relationships, to those favoured by relatively large reductions in resistances.

In these circumstances, where market forces have generated the reductions in resistances, there must be a presumption that patterns of trade are likely to be more economically efficient — that is, drawing supplies from services where costs, after including costs of overcoming objective resistances, are lowest, after the entrepreneurial activity that has led to that restructuring of trade patterns. It is more likely to be analogous to the removal of trade discrimination against the new partner, than to classical trade diversion. Trade may, indeed be "diverted" from old channels to new. It is more likely, however, that the switch will "divert" trade from a less profitable to a more profitable partner. This is not classical "trade diversion". One can imagine circumstances where ignorance or prejudice produces different results, but these are not likely to be common in a competitive market.

The point can be illustrated with one example of considerable contemporary significance. As Taiwan enterprises have put more effort into trade and investment with mainland China in recent years, they have, perforce, devoted less managerial time to identifying and exploiting business ties in the rest of the world. This may have increased absolutely resistances to trade between Taiwan and (parts of) the rest of the world, above what they might otherwise have been, including through economies of scale in overcoming resistances to bilateral trade. But even if it has not, the reduction of resistances to trade between Taiwan and mainland China, in say, labour-intensive electronic components, will have had some effect in diverting trade in these components from other bilateral relationships. This tends to reduce welfare in the rest of the world, unless incomes growth associated with trade creation in Taiwan and China makes these two economies much larger participants in trade with the world as a whole.

The discussion in the preceding paragraphs of "trade diversion" and "trade creation" associated with the reductions in resistances in some but not all bilateral trading relationships, exemplifies a general difference between differential reduction in official and other resistances to trade. Reductions in other resistances result from independent firms' search for lower-cost and more profitable patterns of trade. While the reduction in the gap between minimum possible and actual transport costs may divert trade from old relationships, it is unlikely to divert trade from lower cost to higher cost sources and destinations. Unlike discriminatory reduction in official barriers, it is highly unlikely to reduce welfare in the trading partners experiencing trade expansion or in the world as a whole, although it may still reduce welfare in the rest of the world.

There are externalities associated with investment to reduce **subjective** resistances to trade, and to bring transport and communications costs closer to their **objective** minima. The externalities introduce the possibility of economically efficient roles for government, quite separate from those associated with the reduction of official barriers to trade. They are the rationale for government's providing public goods that are relevant to the efficient operation of an international market: improving transport and communications infrastructure, including through regulatory regimes; reducing perceptions of risk in international contracts; disseminating information on profitable trade opportunities (Garnaut 1991b). The impact of these roles of government on trade and welfare is best analysed in a framework analogous to that applied to independent enterprises' efforts to reduce the cost of resistances, rather than that developed in the pure theory of customs unions for analysis of differentiated reduction in official barriers.

Following Drysdale and Garnaut (1993), this section of the paper has presented elements of a general theory of economic integration. Within this theory, disintegration is the normal condition of inter-regional and international trade in goods and services. The reduction of resistances takes investment and time, and is affected by the whole range of cultural, linguistic, legal and other factors that affect the cost of trade transactions. Much of the dynamism in Asia-Pacific trade expansion derives from the progressive reduction of **subjective**, and **objective** but non-official, resistances to trade. The process has been driven by independent enterprises' search for more profitable patterns of trade, sometimes assisted by provision by governments of "public goods" that affect the operation of private markets.

The general theory of economic integration brings out the crucial distinction between reductions in resistances in some trading relationships through a process of official discrimination, and reductions in resistances through a process of "market" and non-discriminatory integration. Discriminatory integration blocks the economic processes of establishing more profitable patterns of trade.

Where discrimination favours trading relationships that would in any case, through market processes, be large relative to the partner countries' total trade, the chances of economic loss in the partner countries and the world as a whole are correspondingly reduced. These conditions reduce the magnitude of economic loss in the rest of the world. Krugman (1991, 1992) makes this point in relation to adjacent states but draws conclusions beyond those that can be justified by his analysis. Summers (1991) asserts a similar point more strongly, and does not attempt to justify his strong arguments in support of discriminatory liberalization between geographically adjacent economies.

The reality that "optimal" patterns of trade are different across commodities increases the costs of general official discrimination in bilateral trading relationships, for the bilateral partners and the rest of the world. The presence of economies of scale and externalities in overcoming many resistances compounds the effect of trade discrimination in promoting welfare-reducing trade. Discriminatory official barriers block the effects of market pressures in reducing trade resistances in new trading relationships in which investment in building new patterns of trade are justified by changing economic circumstances and opportunities.

V Three Dimensions of Open Regionalism

The analytic framework presented in Sections II to IV suggests three ways in which economic integration can proceed amongst economies in a single region, without discrimination in the application of official barriers to trade.

The first is through non-discriminatory reduction of protection in economies which have the capacity to expand trade as a result of high complementarity, or of low bilateral trade resistances that do not depend on official barriers. Such non-discriminatory trade liberalization may or may not lead to **intensification** of bilateral trade, that is, to faster bilateral trade growth than would be expected from the respective trade expansion of the two economies and the world as a whole (Drysdale and Garnaut 1982).

The second is through expanded provision by governments of public goods relevant to the efficient operation of the regional international market for goods and services (Garnaut 1992; Elek 1992a, 1992b, 1992c). This is likely to intensify regional trade, without any element of discrimination in official barriers.

The third is through the processes of market integration. This can proceed as a result of governments removing official barriers to profit maximizing patterns of trade; or through the dynamics of private discovery of profit maximizing patterns, without any change in the policy stance of governments. Opportunities for expansion of intra-industry and other trade that depends on resistances being low are greater between members of the same geographic region, and especially between adjacent economies, and so market integration is likely to intensify intra-regional trade (Drysdale and Garnaut 1993).

VI Open Regionalism and Reductions in Protection: Prisoners' Dilemma or Prisoners' Delight?

Reductions in official barriers to intra-regional trade promote regional economic integration, and may promote the **intensification** of intra-regional trade, whether or not the liberalization is discriminatory.

As a result, regional economic integration advances in a region of liberalizing economies, and is retarded in a region in which member economies are inward looking and raising barriers to trade. It was the increasingly open character of East Asian economies through the 1970s, with non-discriminatory liberalization in a number of economies expanding opportunities for profitable intra-regional trade, that generated the initial discussion of *open regionalism*. The Asia-Pacific was identified as a region of open economies, in which non-discriminatory, mostly unilateral liberalization was generating rising trade shares of output and expenditure, and rapidly expanding intra-regional trade.

Through the 1980s, and especially from 1985, there was an acceleration of unilateral, non-discriminatory trade liberalization in virtually all market-oriented Western Pacific economies (including China). This led to observation that non-discriminatory trade liberalization was more likely in an economy that was part of a region in which other economies were liberalizing trade, than in a region of increasingly inward-looking states (Garnaut 1991*b*; Drysdale and Garnaut 1993). In this world, each individual economy in a region observes the prosperity others are experiencing as a result of trade liberalization, in which the benefits of each country's liberalization are extended by the contemporaneous liberalization of others. This increases incentives for each country to liberalize its own trade, bringing benefits not only to themselves but to others in the region. In this world, the regional trade policy "game" takes the form of "prisoners' delight", to be contrasted with the "prisoners' dilemma" "game" that has been used to define the process of trade liberalization amongst advanced industrialized economies in recent decades (MacMillan 1991).

The characterization of the trade negotiations "game" as the "prisoners' dilemma" derives from the fact that General Agreement on Tariffs and Trade (GATT) negotiations in practice have been premised on liberalization being a "concession", the withholding of which has value for a member country. There is an incentive to joint and co-operative liberalization, since the perceived gains from the rest of the world's liberalization exceed the perceived costs of one's own liberalization. The perceived pay-off matrix can be stylized along the lines of Table 2.1.

Within the trade policy "game" defined in Table 2.1, the member

TABLE 2.1

Popular Perceptions of Pay-Offs from Unilateral and Joint Liberalization: The "Prisoners' Dilemma"

		Rest of World	
		Liberalize	Protect
Member Country	Liberalize	6, 6	–4, 10
	Protect	10, –4	0, 0

Note: In each cell of the pay-off matrix, the first number is the pay-off to the member country, and the second the pay-off to the rest of the world.

country and the rest of the world, in the absence of co-operation, are driven inexorably to outcomes that are perceived to be less than optimal for all parties. The purpose of trade negotiations within the GATT is to provide a framework in which each member country takes its trade policy decisions in confidence that, if it liberalizes itself, others will liberalize. In a many-country world, there are high costs of organization and enforcement of the framework, unless there is a single, dominant country (a **hegemon**) that can internalize substantial part of the benefits of a successful, jointly liberalizing trade negotiation.

The characterization of trade negotiations as a "prisoner's dilemma" game corresponds to popular perceptions in many countries, as well as to the revealed preferences of many countries. It does, however, sit awkwardly alongside the pay-offs from trade liberalization at home and abroad that are anticipated by standard economic theory. The economist's perceived pay-off matrix can be stylized along the lines of Table 2.2.

To the extent that Table 2.2, presenting insights from economic analysis, represents the reality, each country's unilateral decisions,

TABLE 2.2

Economist's Perception of Pay-Offs from Unilateral and Joint Liberalization: The "Prisoners' Delight"

		Rest of World	
		Liberalize	Protect
Member Country	Liberalize	10, 10	5, 5
	Protect	5, 5	0, 0

Note: In each cell of the pay-off matrix, the first number is the pay-off to the member country, and the second the pay-off to the rest of the world.

to maximize its own welfare, with or without co-operation, leads inexorably towards the best possible outcome for each country and the world as a whole. In these terms, *open regionalism* characterizes a region of open economies, sustained by widespread perceptions that trade liberalization serves the purposes of each member country. There is no requirement of co-operation, and therefore no necessary costs of organization and enforcement, no free rider problem, and no need for a hegemonic leader.

Why do different perceptions of trade liberalization emerge across different regions, supporting such divergent perceptions of trade policy outcomes as presented in Tables 2.1 and 2.2? Polities in which technocratic perceptions of policy outcomes play a larger role in decision-making are more likely to act consistently with the "prisoners' delight" (Table 2.2). Polities in which decision-making processes are more autonomous of sectoral vested interests are more likely to generate the "prisoners' delight".

Perhaps more importantly, observation that trade liberalization has been associated with economic prosperity, historically at home, or contemporaneously abroad, strengthen perceptions that support the "prisoners' delight". This has been important to the emergence and sustenance of *open regionalism* in East Asia. In addition, within a liberalizing region, economic gains from trade liberalization at home will be augmented by gains from trade liberalization abroad. This helps to entrench perceptions that liberalization has generated favourable outcomes.

Tables 2.1 and 2.2 describe polar cases. The reality, even in a liberalizing region, contains elements of both the "prisoners' dilemma" and "prisoners' delight". Perceptions of gains from a member's own liberalization will be somewhat stronger if regional co-operation strengthens perceptions that other countries will liberalize as well.

This differentiated reality is the background to policy analysis and discussion within the Asia-Pacific region, of regional agreements on accelerated trade liberalization on a non-discriminatory basis. This is the new frontier of *open regionalism* in the Asia-Pacific. In an early suggestion along these lines that accepted the "GATT premise" that liberalization would be considered to be a "concession" in the home country, Garnaut (1981) argued that the concentration of high protection in Western Pacific economies in sectors in which other regional economies are the world's lowest cost suppliers, created an opportunity for a set of agreements on sectoral trade liberalization that had prospects for encouraging export expansion for all participating economies, even if liberalization were undertaken on a non-discriminatory basis. This wide spread of "benefits" would facilitate political support for the regional agreements.

Since the entrenchment of the "prisoners' delight" as the dominant trade policy paradigm in the Western Pacific in the second half of the 1980s, non-discriminatory sectoral trade liberalization has been discussed more actively in an APEC-wide framework (Drysdale and Garnaut 1989, 1992; Eagleburger 1992; APEC 1992).

Some recent commentary has incorporated the full logic of the "prisoners' delight", and has argued the desirability of accepting "free-riding" from outside suppliers, including the European Community. Drysdale and Garnaut (1989, 1993) have argued that free-riding, if it occurs, should be accepted by Asia-Pacific economies for the benefits that reducing trade barriers on a most-favoured-nation basis, leading to expansion of APEC markets, provide for members, no matter that it would also help outsiders. They do, however, observe that European "free-riding" on Asia-Pacific agricultural trade liberalization would probably be politically unacceptable if the EC were to subsidize agricultural exports to these markets in the wake of failure to constrain such interventions in a successful Uruguay Round. Krause (1992), more generally, has argued for the application of "conditional MFN" treatment to outsiders seeking to participate in trade expansion deriving from APEC agreements on sectoral trade liberalization.

VII Open Regionalism and Regional Provision of Public Goods

Market exchange requires institutions to define and to enforce property rights and to interpret and enforce contracts. Confidence in the provision of these services is as important as the provision itself. While in some circumstances the operation of the market itself will generate the required institutions, the minimum institutions for market exchange have the character of public goods, and will be underprovided in the absence of action by government.

In addition, efficient market exchange requires mechanisms to internalize externalities in relation to provision of market information, and of physical infrastructure for transport and communications. These services, too, will often be provided economically only in the context of some action by governments.

Many of the institutions for efficient market exchange within sovereign states are provided traditionally by government. Indeed, the institution of government itself grew partly out of requirements for domestic provision of these services. International trade requires similar institutional support for efficient exchange, but there is no international state to play this role (Garnaut 1991b).

Over recent decades, international structures have developed to facilitate international exchange. Some of these, perforce, are closely tuned to the requirements of bilateral and regional rather than global trade. The expansion of institutions to promote optimal supply of public goods to support international exchange is, in its nature, **trade creating**, since the facilitation of trade in additional commodities between new sets of trading partners rarely removes institutions which are supporting established trade. Nevertheless, the finite resources of national governments limit the range of trading relationships that can be serviced fully. Trade will be more intense within relationships — perhaps regional — which have been given highest priority in the provision of institutions that are necessary for international market exchange. In this context, *open regionalism* involves commitment to high levels of provision of institutions to support intra-regional market exchange.

While prosaic in nature, public goods to support international market exchange are of considerable importance. They have been discussed most thoroughly in the work of Elek (1992*a*, 1992*b*, 1992*c*). They provide the core of current discussion of inter-governmental support for Asia-Pacific trade expansion (APEC 1992; PECC 1992).

Understandings on the provision of public goods to support international market exchange are not in their nature exclusive, or discriminatory, although the definition of priorities in their negotiation may introduce elements of *de facto* discrimination. The absence of exclusivity makes them suitable for application to overlapping regional groups, to sub-regional groups involving parts only of two or more countries, or to sub-regional sets of members of wider regional groupings.

VIII Open Regionalism and Market Pressures

So long as government does not erect prohibitive barriers to trade, market processes lead to the reduction over time in resistances to trade. The presence of these processes within regional groupings generates the third of the three sources of *open regionalism*.

There is a sense in which this "market integration" is the purest form of *open regionalism*, since in its nature it contains no element of *de jure* or *de facto* official discrimination. For reasons discussed in Section III, it is rare for reduction of resistances in some trading relationships through market processes to divert trade from more to less profitable channels. Market integration is therefore unambiguously welfare-increasing, for participating countries and the world as a whole.

A liberal general economic environment, extending beyond trade in goods to services, capital, direct foreign investment, information and movements of human skills is important to rapid "market integration". Cultural and language similarity facilitates the reduction in trade resistances through market processes. Low barriers to the reorganization of transport and communications are important, as between adjacent or neighbouring countries. Geographic proximity is important for two types of reasons. It introduces the potential for low **objective** transport and communications costs. And the easy human contact that it facilitates reduces **subjective** resistances.

"Market integration" involves reduction in **subjective** resistances to trade, but builds upon low **objective** resistances. Where proximity within a geographic region is supported by low official barriers, dynamic market processes lead to fine specialization, high levels of intra-industry trade, the establishment of trade-facilitating market institutions and inextricable combinations of movements of goods, services, people and business structures. It is the major source of dynamism in *open regionalism*. But while interpersonal trust and transnational business organization can in favourable circumstances supply some of the public goods that support an efficient international market, the full potential of market integration requires low official barriers, and some inter-governmental support for market exchange.

IX Open Regionalism in the Western Pacific

Open regionalism is important for the United States and the international system first of all because of its contribution to internationally oriented economic growth in East Asia. The reality of *open regionalism* grew in the Western Pacific region alongside its conceptualization, the concept eventually contributing to confidence in internationally oriented growth itself.

All three elements of *open regionalism* have been important in East Asia and the Western Pacific over the past two decades, and especially in the period from 1985, when the margin of superiority of East Asian over world economic performance widened considerably.

The starting point was the adoption of more internationally-oriented growth strategies in one after another East Asian economies. The essence of internationally-oriented strategies is the adoption of trade and industry policies that provide similar incentives for import-competing and export production — that remove the bias towards production for the home market that is associated with traditional protection (Krueger 1980). The economies that have expanded most of all over the past several decades — Singapore and Hong Kong — achieved this balance in incentives through free trade. Japan, Taiwan and Korea at first balanced conventional protection with a range of export subsidies, moving rapidly towards conventional free trade in manufactured goods through the 1970s and 1980s in Japan, and from the mid-1980s in Taiwan and Korea. Several of the other ASEAN states (particularly Malaysia and Thailand) embarked upon trade liberalization from the early 1970s, and all ASEAN economies (although the Philippines less decisively and with less effect) accelerated trade liberalization and internationalization within the dynamics of the "prisoners' delight" in the late 1980s. Australia and New Zealand, which once had the most highly protected manufacturing sectors in the OECD, moved strongly to remove protection from the late 1980s. China removed autarchic bias in its trade and industry policies under the post-1978 economic reforms, particularly with the urban reforms from 1984, and the commitment to build a "socialist market economy" in the years after 1987. The dismantling of political barriers to

China's trade with Taiwan and Korea from about 1987 opened up new areas of rapid trade expansion. Vietnam has implemented economically-oriented economic reform in recent years.

Internationally-oriented economic strategies, and especially trade liberalization from 1985, promoted strong expansion of intra-regional trade, without significant elements of trade discrimination. The open nature of liberalization secured participation in trade expansion from countries outside the Western Pacific which themselves maintained relatively open policies — notably the United States and Canada.

The formation of APEC in 1989, and the new organization's explicit commitment to *open regionalism* strengthened confidence in the dynamics of the "prisoners' delight" in the Western Pacific and provided a channel for its transmission across the Pacific to the United States and Canada. APEC, and a Western Pacific precursor, a series of senior officials meetings on trade policy, were helpful to the binding of its members to a productive outcome from the Uruguay Round. Non-discriminatory sectoral trade liberalization agreements were established in the APEC agenda in 1992, although they have yet to be tested in practice.

The second element of *open regionalism* — co-operation amongst governments to provide public goods essential for efficient international market exchange — has provided useful support to trade liberalization. Recognizing the importance of intra-regional trading links, bilateral economic communications, aid commitments and understanding on open trade and investment became more important. The Sino-British agreement on the future of Hong Kong in 1984 strengthened confidence in cross-border trade and investment ties. This provided the institutional framework for a far-reaching re-specialization of the Hong Kong economy, from supplying relatively labour-intensive manufactured goods to world markets, to high-value services and manufactured inputs to the development and internationalization of the mainland Chinese economy. Economic co-operation amongst the ASEAN states was supported by a widening range of inter-governmental contracts promoting information flows and confidence in the maintenance of open trade policies, prior to the commitment in 1991 to move towards the establishment of a discriminatory free trade area. Inter-governmental understandings on movements of capital, people, information and the provision of transport and communications promoted expansion of trade within sub-regional groups, notably the Johor-Singapore-Batam triangle covering parts of Malaysia, Singapore and Indonesia (Lee 1991). The Closer Economic Relations Agreement between Australia and New Zealand went beyond the establishment of discriminatory free trade towards extensive harmonization of laws and institutions relevant to bilateral trade and investment.

In an environment of confidence that border restrictions on trade and investment were diminishing and would remain low, the third element of *open regionalism* probably made the largest quantitative contribution to intra-regional trade expansion. Direct foreign investment from Japan, and later Taiwan and Korea, especially from the late 1980s, facilitated rapid trade expansion, and the beginnings of intra-industry specialization in manufactured goods production. Economic liberalization supported trade and investment expansion across the Chinese diaspora, from Hong Kong and Taiwan, through Southeast Asia, and back into the mainland of China. The internationalization of the Chinese economy was powerfully supported by the capacity of market processes with an international Chinese community to establish substitutes for the legal security of property rights and contract within the partially reformed mainland economy.

Continued East Asian economic dynamism drew deeply upon, and demonstrated the case for, the emerging *open regionalism.*

The view of a liberalizing East Asia presented in this paper is advisedly at odds with much contemporary North American perception of East Asian economic policy. The empirical basis of this paper's view has been argued extensively elsewhere (Drysdale 1988; Garnaut 1989; Fynmore and Hill 1992).

X Implications for the United States and the International System

Open regionalism has emerged in the Western Pacific as a source of trade and economic dynamism at a time of crisis in the open multilateral trading system. The dynamics of discriminatory regionalism in Europe, under the political and economic strains of deepening institutional integration, and the requirement to accommodate the emergence of market economies in Eastern Europe and the successor states to the Soviet Union, has undermined support for the multilateral system. The United States, the intellectual and political leader of post-war multilateral free trade within the framework of the General Agreement on Tariffs and Trade, is now ambivalent in support of open trade. In the latter part of the Bush Presidency, the United States trade reform energies were allocated first of all to discriminatory trade liberalism in the Americas — at best a third league, behind the multilateral system and Asia-Pacific economic co-operation, in terms of United States and international economic interests. The economics profession in the United States has become nearly as inventive in its justification of discriminatory regionalism and "managed trade" as it once was productive in its support for multilateral open trade. The American political system, under the influence of economic problems which have their origins in domestic policy, has shown itself vulnerable to protectionist pressures.

Open regionalism in the Asia-Pacific provides an opportunity for the United States to renew its commitment to internationally-oriented policies.

Open regionalism in the Western Pacific is a contemporary demonstration of the continuing power of internationally-oriented and market-oriented policies. The value of its demonstration effect is diminished by widespread misperception of the level and tendency of East Asian protection. The value of the demonstration effect would be enhanced by closer engagement with East Asia, politically, economically and intellectually. United States participation in APEC is potentially a crucial instrument of engagement.

Engagement in *open regionalism* in the Asia-Pacific has a second advantage for the political economy of trade policy in the contemporary United States: it brings the renewed legitimacy of regionalism to account in support of open and multilateral policies. When the trade policy choice is explicitly between Pan American regionalism and Asia-Pacific regionalism, the economic calculus points clearly to the Asia-Pacific (Krause 1992). And despite the remembered traditions of the United States' world economic leadership, and the Bush campaign speech in Detroit, regionalism in the Asia-Pacific is now *open regionalism*. There are strong defences against discriminatory regionalism in contemporary East Asia (Drysdale and Garnaut 1993).

There are cross-currents in contemporary United States trade policy sentiment, some of them emerging from reactions to and perceptions of East Asian political economy. "Aggressive unilateralism" turns protectionist sentiment potentially to the service of trade expansion. Its manifestation in bilateral diplomatic pressure and through "Super 301" has yielded some modest successes in East Asian trade policy, but carries large risks to open trade (Bhagwati and Patrick 1991). The successes have been on particular issues where domestic political pressures in East Asia have protected exceptions to the "prisoners' delight", especially with agriculture. The unambiguous successes have brought bilateral pressures to bear in support of GATT disciplines, for example with beef in Korea and Japan. The dangers of aggressive unilateralism are mainly associated with misperceptions of the reality of official trade restriction in East Asia, or of the consequences of genuine liberalization in East Asia. One danger is that the genuine absence of official restriction will mean that no substantive policy response is possible. Another is that, given the origins of United States trade imbalances in domestic fiscal policy, genuinely liberalizing responses will have small, if any, effects on bilateral trade imbalances. In either case, persistent beliefs that policy-related restrictions cause United States trade deficits lead inevitably to disillusionment and increased protectionist pressure, eventually on both sides of the Pacific.

Open regionalism reinforces the GATT-based multilateral system. It is easier to maintain than the GATT-based system, built around resolution of the "prisoners' dilemma", because it makes lesser demands on international leadership. The "prisoners' delight" requires no hegemonic leader. Leadership helps, of course, given the real-world mix of perceptions on trade policy, and the surviving elements of "prisoners' dilemma" in a region structured mainly around "prisoners' delight".

Open regionalism has the major advantage that it can easily accommodate new participants. Latin American states could follow the United States into Asia-Pacific *open regionalism*, depending only on their own capacity to maintain open trade policies. There would be no exclusion of, or disincentive to, the movement towards internationally-oriented strategies, in South Asia or Russia. Perhaps most important of all, it provides an accommodating framework for the eventual re-absorption of Europe into an open trading system.

3
APEC AFTER SEATTLE AND THE URUGUAY ROUND

Introduction

Late in 1993 we all applauded the Clinton Administration's brilliant trade policy triple play: NAFTA through the Congress; the constructive APEC Leaders' Meeting in Seattle; and the successful conclusion to the Uruguay Round by the Congressional deadline. The international economic policy agenda looked much less dangerous, more manageable.

Three months later, the tensions across the Pacific were greater than ever. It seems possible that the United States within a few months will take the unprecedented step of withdrawing most-favoured-nation treatment from a major nation — and an APEC member at that. It seemed possible that the United States within six months would use its unique legislative power to take punitive trade policy action against an APEC member, without reference to the multilateral procedures or consultation within the Asia-

---

This chapter was first presented to a plenary meeting of the Pacific Economic Co-operation Council, Kuala Lumpur, March 1994.

Pacific region. And then, four months after Seattle, it seemed that the two sides of the Pacific, lying in the same bed of commitment to trade liberalization and free trade, discovered that they had different dreams.

How did this state of affairs develop? And what are its implications for APEC after Seattle and the Uruguay Round? Is there a way forward for *open regionalism* and the development of a free trading community in the Asia-Pacific?

To jump ahead of my story: there is a path forward. And the path forward is to be found amongst the ideas that have developed within the networks of the Pacific Economic Co-operation Council (PECC) over the past 14 years. But people who think and worry about development and international relations in all of our countries, and not only our governments, will need to be creative, diligent, and tolerant of imperfection, if we are to keep the history of our region travelling down that path.

It is not surprising that the challenges at this time are large, and the solutions hard. We are living at a unique time in world economic history, when the international community is realizing that the centre of gravity of the world economy has shifted from mid-North Atlantic to mid-Pacific, and continues to shift West. We have just been through the deepest post-war recession in the old industrial economies and — in contrast to all past times — the developing economies of East Asia kept growing, more strongly than ever.

Times of great change are bound to be challenging, interesting, and dangerous. They are bound to keep history running into dead ends and down wrong paths. We can be glad that we put the effort into defining the path before the times were so interesting.

The Economic Shifts

These last few years of recession and slow recovery in North America, then Europe and Japan, are perhaps the most remarkable in the industrialization of East Asia over the past four decades.

East Asian developing economies kept growing through the world recession. As the OECD countries slid into recession, East Asian developing economies grew faster; and went faster still as the industrial economies declined further in 1991. Growth was particularly strong in 1992 and 1993, as Japan plumbed the depths of recession.

The strong performance was widely diffused through the developing economies of East Asia. It was led by the boom in China, defying the intentions of the authorities to ease inflationary pressures, with output increasing by one-quarter in two years. China's boom and import liberalization forced the pace of structural change, which expanded export and investment opportunities throughout the Asia-Pacific region, and most powerfully in Hong Kong, Taiwan and Korea.

Structural change in Hong Kong to meet the opportunity in China kept the economy growing at 5 per cent or more, taking it past the per capita incomes of Britain and Australia, and seemingly defying gravity for an economy in the productivity range of the advanced industrial economies.

Taiwan too, absorbed the structural change of rising incomes and economic liberalization, with the pace forced by the expansion of trade and investment in China. Growth moved to 6 per cent in 1993. Korea has also restored growth in the range of 5–6 per cent after adjusting to the extraordinary political change of the late 1980s.

Just as impressive and more consistent has been the expansion of the ASEAN economies: Malaysia now in its sixth year of growth close to 8 per cent; Thailand close to Malaysian performance; Indonesia entrenching a new pattern of growth based on exports of manufactures; and Singapore now with average incomes in the developed country range, growing as fast as when it was poor and catching up. Vietnam, much poorer than its ASEAN neighbours, has joined the high growth club.

In the Southwest Pacific, Australia and New Zealand, following the pain of structural adjustment to deregulation and trade liberalization, are now growing faster than others in the OECD.

Japan is the odd country out. But the high yen, and the momentum for structural adjustment established by direct investment abroad in more prosperous times, have continued to expand the trade opportunities of its neighbours.

A consistent theme of strong growth in East Asia has been increasing integration into international markets, supported by import liberalization — with exceptions, and sometimes inconsistently over time; but over time, inexorably. Since the mid-1980s imports have grown more rapidly than exports. Current account surpluses of earlier years have disappeared in China (too rapidly) and Korea; and have fallen to moderate proportions in Taiwan.

Again the exception is Japan, whose liberalization and import expansion for manufactured goods helped the current era of rapid growth in developing East Asia to become established in the second half of the 1980s. Macroeconomic misjudgement is now overwhelming the impact of structural change.

Liberalization and strong output and import growth in neighbouring countries have helped each Western Pacific economy to maintain its commitment to growth-oriented policies. East Asian markets have absorbed the majority of East Asian developing economies' export growth since the mid-1980s, explaining the region's resilience through the industrial economies' recession.

Sustained, rapid economic growth has allowed East Asian economies to catch up with advanced industrial economies more quickly than the simple arithmetic of measured per capita GDP and rates of growth suggests. Once labour becomes scarce, continued rapid growth and structural change rapidly increase incomes and the real exchange rate. This is the harvest time of East Asian style growth, as measured per capita income rises rapidly from about US$5,000 to the frontiers of the advanced economies. This is the stage of development of Hong Kong and Singapore through the 1980s, of Taiwan and Korea currently, and soon Malaysia. It is a time of national self confidence, and of expanding ambitions of individual citizens.

The most dramatic change is in China, now growing faster than any of its neighbours in their periods of strong growth. Awkwardly, and with risks of macroeconomic and social instability. But powerfully, and despite disruptions, inexorably. By appropriate measures already the world's fourth largest economy, China will be the third by the end of the century. By then the East Asian economy, appropriately measured, will be substantially larger than the North American or Western European.

These are the changes that are behind the divergent perspectives on trade policy and regional co-operation on the two sides of the Pacific. Commonly, even professional perceptions on both sides of the Pacific lag behind the reality of growing economic power and self confidence in East Asia. Americans underestimate the corrosion of their overwhelming power, and their capacity to lead by fiat. East Asians underestimate the expansion of their influence on the international system, and their responsibility for systemic leadership.

Open Regionalism: Same Bed, Different Dreams

At Seattle, Heads of Government did not endorse the Eminent Persons Group visionary recommendation on working towards free trade in the Asia-Pacific region. In a meeting of huge significance and benefit for regional co-operation, this was one issue that did not come together on cue.

The absence of endorsement did not amount to a rejection of the free trade objective. It followed from different conceptions of the requirements for free trade, and of the means of securing free trade. These different dreams were carried forward into the Leaders' meeting from the Eminent Persons Group itself. They relate to substantial issues that cannot be finessed; which must be worked through and resolved, before the Asia-Pacific Economic Community can deliver on the ambitions for it that we share.

One modern American dream is of a free trade area, of the Americas, from Alaska to Terra del Fuego; which forms the base of a PAFTA, I suppose from Maine and the Maritimes to Medan and Melbourne.

This is not an old American dream. The old dream was multilateral free trade, as participants in the first Pacific Trade and Development Conference learned in Tokyo a quarter of a century ago.

But tides turn, and there is no doubting the depth of the new tide of NAFTA-style regionalism in the United States. It is not an aberration of the new administration. The Clinton Administration legislated Bush's NAFTA, and it was President Bush's campaign speech in Detroit in September 1992 that first sent the shock waves of discriminatory regionalism westward across the Pacific. The United States polity, having supported the international system within which one after another Western Pacific economies transformed themselves from poverty into successful industrial economies, has now decided that it has had enough. The United States then was incomparably dynamic, successful and strong. It now feels defensive, and blames the failure of others to play the free market game. It supports free trade, it says; but only if others are opening their markets, and conditionally upon concessions by others.

Cornered by PECC and APEC commitments to *open regionalism*, the American proponents of NAFTA-style regionalism say that the arrangements will be open to any economy that will make reciprocal commitments. It is politically more realistic, the proponents say, because the polities of large economies simply will not tolerate the benefits of their own liberalization extending to countries that have not made reciprocal 'concessions'. It is better for free trade, they add, because it will encourage or force a wider range of countries to lower their protection.

This perception of the political constraints is a fair description of the contemporary political economy of the United States. It is a long way from the mark as a description of the contemporary political economy of the Western Pacific, as experience since the mid-1980s attests in Japan, Taiwan and Korea (each for manufactured goods, but only minimally for agriculture and some services); China; each of the ASEAN countries; Australia and New Zealand. This different reality is not well understood in the United States; and I wonder if the American political constraints on unconditional most-favoured-nation liberalization would bind as tight if it were better known.

Still, for the foreseeable future, it is part of the real world in which Asia-Pacific economies must shape their trade policies, that the United States will not happily be part of regional liberalization that admits free riding by significant economies.

PECC has developed a different dream. It is not only an East Asian or Western Pacific dream, because Americans have been principals to its development over these past 14 years. But it is currently a dream that does not pass through the mind of the American political mainstream.

The PECC dream is of a region of free trading countries, avoiding discrimination amongst themselves or against outsiders. It is of a region of deepening economic integration, in which markets and business enterprises, rather than official institutions are the main agents of change. Governments support economic integration through the provision of social, political and physical infrastructure of various kinds, but along the contours shaped by dynamic markets. It is of a region of growing, successful, self-confident economies, recognizing that they themselves are principal beneficiaries of their own liberalization, and that if others grow better through opportunities deriving from their own liberalization then this does no harm. It is of a region that sees the benefits of trade liberalization and shares the ambition of creating a region in which all trade is free, but which recognizes that there are particular practical constraints in particular countries that will make progress uneven.

This, of course, is partly the reality as well as the dream of recent economic integration and growth in the Western Pacific. Within PECC, participants have identified important ways in which the reality can more fully reflect the dream. APEC is crucial to this alignment of reality with vision. APEC leaders gave crucial momentum to the Uruguay Round settlement last December, and can help to keep implementation on track. Confidence in a shared ultimate goal or a community of free trade helps each participant to maintain trade liberalization momentum, in its own national interest but against pressures from domestic vested interests. There will be some issues in which groups of APEC members find it easier to accelerate liberalization together than alone, extending the expanded access on an unconditional most-favoured-national basis. Each element of the APEC Trade and Investment Program promises opportunities to expand real trade and economic integration: on customs procedures; investment issues; standards. The experience of market integration in the Asia-Pacific tells us that these are substantial matters, as important to trade expansion as tariff reductions negotiated eyebrow to eyebrow in Geneva.

We should be clear that virtually all APEC members supported the Clinton Administration's efforts to have Congress pass the NAFTA legislation not because NAFTA embodies good trade principles, or because it will help trade expansion across the Pacific. It does not and will not. NAFTA set up defensive tremors across the Pacific. Rather, APEC members in the Western Pacific wanted Congress to pass NAFTA because the Clinton Administration's defeat would have damaged those elements with the continuing commitment to free trade in the American polity.

The PECC and Western Pacific doubts about NAFTA-style regionalism — about conditional most- favoured-nation treatment with its discrimination against outsiders — have several elements. First of all, it is impractical on a Pacific-wide basis. In the year that the United States is threatening to withdraw most-favoured-nation treatment from China for reasons unrelated to the trade regime, is it realistic to contemplate Chinese access to United States' markets, not only on the same basis as all trading countries, but free? Who would anticipate the support of an American Congress, elements of which are pressing the use of Super 301 against Japan, for free trade with Japan? Neither would it be helpful to the continuation of liberalization of highly protected markets in some APEC members, including China, Indonesia and the Philippines, to enter the bureaucratic tit for tat that characterized United States negotiations with Canada.

NAFTA is simply impractical in the Asia-Pacific. But more than that, it would be undesirable if it were practical. It would make it harder not easier, for non-members including India, Vietnam and Russia, to launch successfully the market-oriented reforms in which APEC members recognize powerful interests, and to which India and Vietnam, at least, are committed. The clumsy rules of origin and the exceptions of the NAFTA would tangle the webs of intra-industry specialization across borders that now characterize the manufacturing and service industries in dynamic economies.

While selective Western Pacific rather than APEC-wide membership of NAFTA would be seductive to some, it would be even more damaging to Asia-Pacific dynamism. Who can imagine Taiwan or Korea trading freely into NAFTA, restricting use of mainland Chinese inputs for reasons of rules of origin? Or Thailand allowing duty free access for American but not Japanese consumer goods? NAFTA-style discriminatory regionalism is a pipe dream from old Shanghai.

The PECC dream of *open regionalism* is practical, because we have seen it at work, and can see how it can go further. But it is not only practical. It is better than old-style regionalism in the mode of the EU and NAFTA, for its members and the rest of the world.

Bringing America In

What to do about the alternative vision and the political constraints across the North Pacific? And what is the prospect of conserving the framework of *open regionalism* in the face of deterioration of United States relations with China and Japan, and prospectively on similar issues with one or more of the ASEAN countries? How to handle an aggrieved state in the Asia-Pacific system, which happens to be most powerful politically, militarily and still economically?

How to bring the United States into the PECC dream?

It is important for America to participate. The United States was the original architect and guarantor of the trading system within which East Asian dynamism emerged. It is still an important source of strength for the global framework of that system, and a better source of strength if integrated closely with the Western Pacific. The trade and investment links across the Pacific are immense and growing still and any weakening of them would seriously shrink the fabric of Asia-Pacific economic co-operation. The United States' security role remains important for political stability in Northeast Asia, and a weakening of economic ties could destabilize political relationships, not least on the Korean peninsular.

It is important for Western Pacific states to recognize the

greater responsibilities of leadership in system development and maintenance that arise from their increased economic power. It will be costly if Western Pacific states hesitate in implementation of Uruguay Round commitments, and productive if they are able to move ahead of commitments. Most Western Pacific states are preparing the implementation of various next steps in trade liberalization following the progress of recent years. It will be greatly to the advantage of trans-Pacific relations, and Asia-Pacific economic co-operation, if these steps are taken early and in advance of external pressure. This is particularly important in Japan, where an appearance of incapacity to liberalize except in response to pressure has grown from tardiness on high-profile issues, and obscured the reality of radical liberalization, structural change and import growth in manufactured goods since the mid-1980s.

A second step, growing out of the first, is to extend more widely into the United States political consciousness an appreciation of the extent of East Asian liberalization and import expansion in recent years. This is a necessary precursor to the expansion of understanding of and support for the PECC vision of *open regionalism*. A third step is for Western Pacific states to accept that this is not a likely time for trade liberalization in the United States, beyond current multilateral commitments. Steps in concerted liberalization in the Asia-Pacific in the period ahead are worthwhile even if there is minimal United States participation. If the United States benefits as a free rider, so much the better. Over time this will help the American appreciation of trade liberalization in the Western Pacific.

What the Western Pacific can reasonably ask of the United States within Asia-Pacific Economic Cooperation is genuine commitment to the rules and spirit of the multilateral system, and consultation within APEC on proposed departures from them. The withdrawal of most-favoured-nation treatment from one country is a threat to the multilateral system as well as to Asia-Pacific

Economic Cooperation. The same can be said of unilateral punitive action under Super 301. There would be no neat containment of the consequences of such action to United States bilateral relations with particular countries. It would bring havoc and the dogs of war to the whole region.

What Is to Be Done?

What is APEC to do after Seattle and the Uruguay Round?

The first thing is to have confidence in the PECC vision of an Asia-Pacific community of economies that are integrating more closely through market processes. Confidence in a community, the member governments of which are committed to an eventual goal of free trade, and taking their opportunities to move towards it, without feeling constrained to match each step to others. A community in which governments are working purposefully to reduce transactions costs on trade and investment, first of all through pressing ahead with the elements of the APEC Trade and Investment Work Programme, and going further as opportunities present themselves. A community that recognizes the value to itself of trade liberalization and expansion, without resenting the benefits that others derive from it.

This is in no way a second rate conception of free trade. It is no failure of vision to prefer it to the conventional style of free trade area, in the form of the EU or NAFTA. It is PECC's and the Asia-Pacific's own invention, which has proven itself in the most important episode of trade expansion and economic growth that the world has ever seen.

The second thing is to respond to United States disillusionment with open trade, with leadership in system development and trade liberalization from the Western Pacific.

The third is to dig deeper within the framework of *open regionalism*, into opportunities for accelerating liberalization through concerted action. Here there is promise in current efforts to identify sectors where liberalization on an unconditional most-favoured-nation basis would have large effects in expanding trade amongst APEC members. Other members should have minimal expectations of new United States commitments, for the time being. The United States leadership of the international system was crucial to the establishment of internationally-oriented industrialization in East Asia. The shift of economic power towards East Asia has occurred with such speed and on such a scale, that it is inevitable that the United States should take time to adapt to new realities. It is important for all APEC countries that the United States remains linked to the Western Pacific through the process of adaptation.

One last word in the manner of acknowledgement for our hosts.

Malaysia is an exemplar of East Asian style trade expansion and development. Malaysia's success allows it to view generously the difficulties of others. The tensions in United States relations with several East Asian states are a spur and temptation to defensive conceptions of East Asian co-operation. The Malaysian idea of an East Asian Economic Caucus can help to build expansively support for *open regionalism* on the PECC model. This generous conception of the Caucus might be encouraged if its boundaries were defined by commitment to an idea and an ideal, rather than by ethnicity. I would hope that consideration could be given to participation by Southwest Pacific states who shared East Asian commitment to genuine, non-discriminatory *open regionalism*.

4

OPTIONS FOR ASIA-PACIFIC TRADE LIBERALIZATION
A Pacific Free Trade Area?

I Asia-Pacific Economic Community and Co-operation

Asia-Pacific Economic Co-operation (APEC) is two things.

It is first of all the Asia-Pacific economic community: the community of relatively and increasingly open and rapidly growing economies, deeply and increasingly integrated with each other, benefiting from large and expanding economic relations with the rest of the world. It is a community built by independent enterprises operating in markets, and not by governments. It is a community that reveals itself and defines its own boundaries through its economic characteristics and interactions, and not through the assertion of a collective international political will (Drysdale 1988; Frankel 1993). Its members conduct about 71 per cent of their trade with each other — a similar ratio to that within Western Europe, despite the relative absence of preferential arrangements

---

This chapter was first presented at a seminar on Asia-Pacific Economic Co-operation at the Institute of Southeast Asian Studies in Singapore in June 1994.

among Asia-Pacific states. Trade intensity — a more relevant measure — is higher in intra-APEC than intra-EC trade (Drysdale and Garnaut 1993).

APEC is secondly a process of inter-governmental Asia-Pacific Economic Co-operation, which aims to conserve, strengthen and extend the older Asia-Pacific economic community. This second manifestation of APEC began with twelve members at the ministerial meeting in Canberra in 1989. It was expanded to include the three Chinese economies in Northeast Asia in Seoul in 1992. APEC assumed increased weight with the informal meeting of leaders in Seattle in 1993, and the agreement to include Papua New Guinea, Mexico and Chile.

The Eminent Persons Group (EPG) recommended to the Seattle ministerial meeting that the inter-governmental APEC be renamed the Asia-Pacific Economic Community (Eminent Persons Group 1993). Ministers were initially cautious about the potential for misunderstanding. They were concerned that the change might foreshadow the building of an Economic Community in the European style. It is clear now that this is not a possibility, and the merging of the two meanings of APEC might be helpful in binding the second to the service of the first.

The Asia-Pacific economic community is a huge success, underpinning sustained growth and prosperity in countries that were amongst the poorest on earth one and two generations ago. It has taught the global community about new, more productive approaches to development strategy and regional integration (Drysdale and Garnaut 1993).

APEC, too, is accumulating achievements, with three large successes already in these early years. First, recognizing the way in which external benefits associated with private activities place limits on the extent to which individual enterprises can provide the institutional and physical infrastructure of regional exchange, APEC has made progress towards Asia-Pacific *trade and investment facilitation*. The Asia-Pacific experience has demonstrated realities that previously were unrecognized or under-valued: that reductions in costs of international transactions, separately from barriers imposed by governments at the borders of their countries, can have powerful trade-expanding effects; and that inter-governmental co-operation in the provision of public goods and services can help to reduce transactions costs. The first report of the Eminent Persons Group (EPG) in 1993 recommended a programme of trade facilitation, and there is now substantial momentum in development of the programme. If the current momentum is maintained and converted progressively into policy action, it will be of large significance — warranting the attention and pride of presidents and prime ministers. It is in the nature of the issues on the trade facilitation agenda — convergence of standards, dispute settlement procedures, an investment code and so on — that they involve no necessary discrimination against outsiders, unlike the old style free trade area or customs union.

APEC's second success was its contribution to the successful conclusion of the Uruguay Round, through consistent support for multilateral liberalization, and through an understanding at the eleventh hour in Seattle on new offers from Asia-Pacific economies.

APEC's third success was to catch the eye of the United States at a time of the latter's preoccupation with domestic policy problems in the first eighteen months of the new Clinton Administration, increasing awareness in the United States of the costs of unproductive tensions in its economic relations with Western Pacific states. This provided significant support for those in the United States who argued for the abandonment or modification of policy positions that promised calamity in trans-Pacific relations and for the wider Asia-Pacific community — the issue of most-favoured-nation (MFN) trade with China, the issues of quantitative targets and bilateral sanctions with Japan, and the linking of trade and labour issues in relations with developing East Asian economies, especially with ASEAN.

APEC in these early years is groping towards more precise definition of its character and role. APEC was formed on the principle of *open regionalism,* the minimal interpretation of which is that it involves regional trade liberalization in a way that does not disadvantage other countries. Japan's nominee in the EPG, Ippei Yamazawa, has written of APEC as an *Open Economic Association* (Yamazawa 1992), and has received considerable support around the region (Keating 1993): *open* in the sense of acting only in ways that strengthen multilateral roles and institutions, and that reduce barriers to trade both within the region and with the rest of the world; *economic* in avoiding explicitly security affairs; and an *association* in the sense of staying away from the creation of an international authority, or binding agreements, or negotiations on issues that do not lend themselves to voluntary agreement by all parties.

This was the spirit of the Vision Statement of APEC leaders in Seattle in November 1993. APEC leaders recognized that the foundation of the region's dynamism was the multilateral trading system. They noted the movement towards interdependence among Asia-Pacific economies, and the growing sense of community. They envisioned a community of Asia-Pacific economies premised on finding co-operative solutions to the challenges thrown up by economic change. They sought continued reduction in trade and investment barriers to support expansion of trade with each other and the world, so that "goods, services, capital and investment flow freely among our economies". Leaders welcomed the challenge to achieve free trade in the Asia-Pacific and to advance global liberalization; and committed APEC to strengthening trade and investment liberalization in the region and facilitating regional co-operation in such areas as standards.

There are obvious ambiguities at the boundaries of these

concepts and statements. But within these boundaries there is a strong foundation of carefully considered and agreed positions, from which the Asia-Pacific economic community can grow more productively. The secure and agreed agenda of APEC can make an important difference, independently of the further definition of issues beyond the boundaries (Elek 1992*a*).

This chapter discusses the potential for APEC to enhance the beneficent processes that have created the Asia-Pacific community, beyond the uncontroversial but potentially highly productive trade and investment facilitation agenda. The next section discusses some recent tendencies in trade and development within the community that have implications for its future development and for the role of inter-governmental co-operation. Section III addresses trade liberalization in the member economies of APEC, including its practical limits. A Pacific Free Trade Area (PAFTA), suggested by the history of regionalism in Europe and North America, is an impractical idea in the Asia-Pacific, with the potential to undermine the momentum of co-operation in productive areas, and even to stall the older processes of expansion of Asian Pacific economic relations. APEC can nevertheless be helpful to trade liberalization through other means, as discussed in Section IV. Section V sums up the future agenda for APEC.

II New Trends in Asia-Pacific Development

The remarkable story of sustained rapid economic growth and deepening international economic integration in the Asia-Pacific region since World War II is now well known (Garnaut and Drysdale 1994). It has dug new and deeper channels over the past decade, and again through the recent period of recession and slow recovery in the OECD economies. The new channels have implications for APEC.

The early heavy reliance of export-oriented growth in East

Asia on the U.S. market intensified in the first half of the 1980s, as loose fiscal and tight monetary policies drove up the foreign exchange-value of the U.S. dollar. This era ended with the trans-Pacific adjustments in fiscal policy and exchange rates following the Plaza Accord in 1985. Since then the greater part of East Asian export growth has been to other East Asian economies, although the U.S. market remains absolutely very important. Real appreciation of the currencies of high income East Asian economies — first and most dramatically Japan, but also Hong Kong, Singapore, Taiwan and South Korea — opened opportunities for others in their own and third country markets. These developments were strengthened by major trade liberalization in the manufacturing sectors of Japan, Taiwan and Korea, mostly unilaterally as measures of domestic economic adjustment, but in some industries helped along by pressure from the United States. Export growth in those lower-income East Asian economies that had implemented internationally-oriented policies was supported by foreign direct investment (FDI) from the higher-income economies in labour-intensive industries that had lost competitiveness at home. Liberalization of import and FDI regimes in East Asian developing economies facilitated regional adjustment — in Malaysia and Thailand, and with powerful effect in Indonesia and China — in all cases unilaterally for reasons of domestic economic strategy.

Most remarkable of all in this period was the rapid emergence of China as a major player in the Asia-Pacific economy, as an importer, exporter and recipient of direct and portfolio foreign investment. China's commitment to reform of state enterprises and the urban economy in 1984, a "planned socialist market economy" in 1987, and a "socialist market economy" in 1992 were landmarks in Chinese domestic economic strategy. The growth in confidence in Hong Kong-China business relations after the Sino-British agreement of 1984, and the progressive easing of official restrictions on economic transactions with Taiwan and South Korea from

1987 supported rapid and deep integration of the Chinese economy with its East Asian near neighbours.

Breaking the chains of historical precedents, the East Asian developing economies continued to grow strongly in the early 1990s despite OECD recession and slow recovery, even through the sharp decline in Japanese output in 1993. The weighted average growth in output in developing East Asia was particularly strong in 1992 (9.5%), and 1993 (10.1%). Structural adjustment and high levels of direct investment from Japan, with further yen appreciation offsetting the effects of recession, supported export-oriented growth in developing East Asia. The fortuitous timing of the heights of the China boom in 1992 and 1993, coincidentally with recession in Japan, expanded opportunities for respecialization in higher value activities in Hong Kong, Taiwan and South Korea, and to some extent in Southeast Asia. Southeast Asian economies experienced strong growth in 1992 (6.1%) and 1993 (6.9%), despite OECD recession and anxiety that the flood of direct and portfolio investment to China would divert investment from other East Asian developing economies.

The impact of Chinese liberalization and growth on Asia-Pacific economies has sparked realization over the past two years that China is a much larger economy than suggested by the official domestic and international data. Work at the Australian National University indicates that if Chinese incomes and output were valued in a way that was comparable with other low-income developing economies, real output would be about three times official levels, making China the world's fourth largest as well as most rapidly growing economy (Garnaut and Ma 1993; Garnaut and Huang 1994).

Trade and economic liberalization and the associated growth in output and foreign economic relations in East Asia have had important implications for economic strategy and structure in the high-income, English-speaking economies of the Asia-Pacific region: Australia, New Zealand, the United States and Canada. Since the late 1980s, all have come to see export growth as a key component of strategies to lift economic performance, and all have assigned East Asian markets a key role in export-oriented strategy. Australia responded first and most strongly to the East Asian opportunity. Australia and New Zealand supported export-oriented strategies with radical unilateral liberalization of payments and trade. The response in North America has been more ambiguous: initially a more open economy, the United States increased protection through the 1980s, but committed itself to remove the new barriers and go further in liberalizing imports in the context of the Uruguay Round. NAFTA raised questions about trade policy in relation to the Western Pacific, some of which were answered positively by the successful conclusion of the Uruguay Round. All four English-speaking economies have experienced strong growth in manufactured and service exports to East Asia since the mid-1980s. All four have experienced relatively early and strong recovery from the OECD recession.

The success of export-oriented growth in East Asia has been influential beyond its earlier boundaries, in some cases beyond the current APEC membership. Within the East Asian region itself, Vietnam launched itself upon a course of economic reform including trade and investment liberalization in the late 1980s, and in the early 1990s has enjoyed high growth of output and exports in the East Asian style. After several false starts, the Philippines since 1992 has made the most promising of its attempts at economic reforms to enter East Asian-style export-oriented growth. Outside East Asia, India, released ideologically and strategically by the collapse of the Soviet planned economy, has been strongly influenced by East Asian (notably Chinese) success, and has embarked on a programme of economic reform including unilateral trade and payments liberalization, that holds promise of substantially stronger economic and trade growth. India's South Asian neighbours are following similar courses. The four major South Asian economies (that is, including Pakistan, Bangladesh, and Sri Lanka) will come to interact closely with the Asia-Pacific economic community. In Latin America, too, East Asian export-oriented growth has been noticed and is emulated, most decisively in Chile.

These developments in the Asia-Pacific and world economies over the past decade have important implications for APEC. Changes in the membership of APEC and extensions of export-oriented growth strategies into Vietnam and South Asia, mean that it is more important than ever that APEC be open at its boundaries, avoiding any discrimination against outsiders. It is more obvious now than ever before that the framework of APEC must be capable of accommodating a huge, rapidly changing Chinese economy: any tendency to define core APEC activities in a way that created difficulties for full Chinese participation would render APEC less relevant and probably counter-productive. And the change in the focus of trade expansion towards East Asia means that East Asian attitudes to and conceptions of the regional trade regime must be influential in the shaping of APEC if it is to be durable and effective. It is no longer realistic for the region to take its economic policy cue from Washington.

Within the economies that are members of APEC there is a strong record of recent trade liberalization or, in the case of North America, commitment to liberalization in the context of the Uruguay Round. There is strong growth momentum in most parts of the region. Papua New Guinea and the Philippines stand out as weak spots in the region's economic development. Otherwise the problems of economic stagnation and poverty are mostly intra-country — the inland of China, Indonesia away from the industrial cities, the Northeast of Thailand. Important although these weak spots are to the communities involved, they are less than overwhelming in relative size — even in China (Riskin 1996). The building of an Asia-Pacific economic community around the movement of goods, services and capital will require APEC as an institution to give attention to these weak spots in development, and to provide a place on its agenda for development co-operation.

III Trade Liberalization: A Pacific Free Trade Area?

The hard and controversial issues in APEC since the 1993 EPG Report, and the leaders' meeting in Seattle, relate to "free trade".

APEC leaders in Seattle were clear in their commitments to reduce barriers so that "goods, services, capital and investment flow freely among our economies", and in welcoming the challenge to achieve free trade in the Pacific. Leaders endorsed the EPG Report's ambitious programme of trade facilitation, and the strong recommendations on support for the multilateral trading system, but not the recommendations to "adopt an ultimate goal of free trade in the region" and to "determine in 1996 the timetable and strategy for reaching that goal".

The rejection of the free trade recommendations was not a rejection of the goal of free trade amongst Asia-Pacific economies. This is clear from the Leaders' vision statement. The superiority of export-oriented strategies to countries that pursue them, and the essential part that open trade and payments plays in export-oriented strategies, are now well understood in policy-relevant circles throughout the Western Pacific. There is no longer principled assertion that any alternative is superior to free trade.

There is, however, deep and principled division within the Asia-Pacific region about the appropriate and precise content of "free trade", the trade policies towards third countries that would accompany free trade amongst Asia-Pacific economies, the practicality and desirability of various means and rates of progress to free trade, and the implications of formal agreement on the goal of free trade. Above all, there are conflicting visions of the role of trade discrimination, within APEC transitionally along the way to eventual APEC-wide free trade, and against outsiders, at least during an indefinite period awaiting reciprocal liberalization.

The conflict is reflected in ambiguity in the 1993 EPG Report. But the conflict was not created by the Report. There is a real conflict of visions of free trade, which for the moment is shading the large area of common ground amongst APEC members on trade liberalization.

It is a spectre, of APEC as an old-style free trade area, a Pacific Free Trade Area (PAFTA), which discriminates against outsiders, and against APEC members that do not meet the PAFTA tests, that is throwing the shadow.

The principal proponent of discriminatory free trade within APEC, Fred Bergsten, Chairman and U.S. nominee, has acknowledged recently that the 1993 Report did not propose a discriminatory free trade area, but rather "free trade within the area" (Bergsten 1994). He argues, nevertheless, that "free trade within the area" on a non-discriminatory basis is impractical and undesirable. It is impractical because in allowing "free riding" by outsiders, including in large trading entities such as the European Union, it "would run afoul of domestic political realities in the United States and most other APEC members". It is undesirable because it would provide no incentive for outsiders to negotiate multilaterally. Bergsten discusses the possibility of extension of discriminatory free trade within parts of the APEC area, for example through some but not all Western Pacific members joining NAFTA; but notes that the EPG concluded that such a course

> would be inferior to progress encompassing all of APEC because it would generate new discrimination within the region during a possibly long transition period.

Bergsten nevertheless expresses the view that, failing APEC-wide discriminatory free trade (a full PAFTA), a partial PAFTA is better than none.

The practicality and desirability of non-discriminatory free trade, or practical progress towards it, is discussed in Section IV. The focus here is on the desirability and practicality of the full or partial PAFTA proposals themselves.

The main issues have been much discussed, and are now well known (Drysdale and Garnaut 1989, 1993).

The first point is that it would be unrealistic at this stage for at least several major economies that are members of APEC to commit themselves to clean free trade with APEC as a whole. The point can be made by reference to the region's two most populous economies.

China has experienced a faster rate of trade liberalization over the past decade than any other country. No other centrally planned economy in transition has so far moved so successfully and so rapidly. And yet there is a huge distance to be travelled. A debate about relaxation of old commitments to self-sufficiency in grain has begun, but inevitably, in the best of circumstances, will be a long time in delivering full integration into international markets. Even in sectors where the policy debate has been won for open trade, the purely practical problems, impervious to the strongest exercise of political will, will slow progress for quite some time, for example, in some areas where reform of state enterprises must precede genuinely free trade. There is little doubt regarding China's ultimate success in market-oriented reform and integration into international markets; but it would be fantasy for a Chinese government to commit itself to clean free trade in one or two decades, or for foreign governments to act on the basis of any commitments to that effect that China might give.

In the United States, the impracticality of commitment to APEC-wide free trade has two dimensions. The first is that it is unrealistic to expect U.S. commitment to clean free trade with

APEC members. Even the comparatively modest adjustment problems of clean free trade with Canada and Mexico proved to be beyond the capacity of the U.S. polity: the exceptions associated with agriculture alone make the point. Would it be easier to allow free entry of Australian sugar and beef? On textiles and clothing, the heavily compromised commitments in the Uruguay Round proved to be difficult enough. Can the political economy of the U.S. Congress support the opening of its market to free entry for textiles and clothing from China, after all the trauma associated with the recent acceptance that China's products should be allowed, not free entry, but the same constrained access as the rest of the world? The second dimension of the U.S. problem is that the American polity is in no mood to accept the bona fides of major East Asian countries' commitment to open trade, even when the realities support the case. The removal of most Japanese official border restrictions on trade in manufactured goods inspired a search for hidden barriers, some real and some imagined, in institutions that are beyond the reach of any simple exercise of political will by the Japanese Government. Since it would be the perception and not the reality of East Asian reciprocity that would be relevant to U.S. policy-making, is it a real possibility that Japan, or China, or Indonesia would pass the test? The Administration's report to the Congress on future free trade areas underlines the difficulties and, at this time, the impossibility of the U.S. accepting free trade with some East Asian members of APEC.

APEC leaders were wise in Seattle, and would be wise again, to avoid committing themselves to an unrealistic vision. Failure to deliver upon commitments would damage the credibility of the leaders themselves, and of APEC, and unleash disappointment, bitterness, and recrimination, with profound and unpredictable consequences.

Recognition of the impracticality of commitment in the foreseeable future to APEC-wide free trade area has led to proponents of discriminatory arrangements into a search for a partial PAFTA. Why not a free trade area amongst "18 minus X" economies, where X is the number of economies that are now unable to commit to free trade with other APEC members? As an officer of the Japanese Foreign Ministry commented recently, "one trouble is that X would be a very large number; 1.3 billion for a start!" Japanese perceptions of contemporary geo-strategic realities would not allow China nor any ASEAN member, to be X alone.

The consequences of a partial free trade area that excluded Japan, or China, or Indonesia, or ASEAN as a whole, would be calamitous for the Asia-Pacific economic community. It would be equally calamitous if the dynamics of negotiation and rising tension led the East Asian economies to the view that it was less disruptive for X to be North America. It would take no more than serious discussion of a partial PAFTA between two or more governments of the region's major countries (the United States, China, Japan and Indonesia or ASEAN) to set in train a process of beggar-thy-neighbour negotiations that would lead to the destruction of productive but fragile APEC.

A variation on the "18 minus X" theme, is that negotiations on the establishment of a free trade area could proceed sector by sector, with X countries that are not able to reciprocate in a particular sector being denied the benefits of other's liberalization in this sector. On the face of it, this would violate Article 24 of the GATT, which requires that free trade should cover substantially all of the trade of the area.

Why not allow longer transition periods for economies that face greater difficulties in implementing free trade? There are two problems. First, it would not solve the problem of perceptions in the U.S. polity: would Congress accept free entry of Chinese or Indonesian products soon, on the basis of a promise of reciprocity much later? More fundamentally, it is unwise to start now upon a path the end of which is now out of sight, with differences in perceptions of what is feasible and desirable. In conclusion, PAFTA is not a practical possibility; and great practical damage would be done by beginning to act out a fantasy.

PAFTA would be undesirable even if it were a practical possibility. It would be undesirable because it would place barriers in the path of market-oriented reform in countries the success of which is of strategic significance to APEC members: Vietnam, of great importance to the ASEAN states at least; and India, struggling in the early stages of reform; and Latin America beyond Mexico and Chile. Even if there were no increase in APEC economies' barriers against outsiders, the new reformers — Vietnam, India, and so on — would find that they were competing on much less favourable terms than before against their main competitors in their main markets and potential markets.

Could not the reforming outsiders be offered membership? In each case, the practical difficulties in reciprocating free trade would be at least as large as with China or Indonesia.

Could the members of APEC, or APEC minus X, be left free to choose whether they liberalize on a discriminatory or non-discriminatory basis? ASEAN could then allow free access for Vietnam; and North America for the Latin states; and East Asia for India. A positive response to this question would raise more questions. If the practical politics of trade liberalization in the United States requires reciprocity and the absence of free riders, would this leave sufficient reciprocity and no surfeit of free riding? If the answer were yes, the non-discriminating members' trade and specialization with outsiders would still tangle with the discriminating members' rules of origin. And penalties in the markets of the discriminating economies would still be an unwelcome inhibition for market-oriented change in the reforming outsiders. To be consistent with Article 24, of the GATT, the selected outsiders as well as the APEC members (or APEC minus X) would need to enter a full, reciprocal free trade area with the APEC country granting the special treatment and with each other.

There is one other large reason why PAFTA is undesirable. Trade liberalization has proceeded steadily and sometimes swiftly in Asia-Pacific economies over the past decade, and is set to make new progress as the Uruguay Round is implemented and China prepares for entry into the World Trade Organization (WTO). Indonesia has also announced major new steps on liberalization of foreign direct investment. If the APEC members enter negotiations to establish a formal free trade area, the focus will shift from the benefits of unilateral liberalization to the rules of the new game. It would be most surprising if momentum were not lost in the productive processes that have been binding the Asia-Pacific economic community more closely in recent years, and that promise even more in the period during which Uruguay Round commitments are implemented.

IV Trade Liberalization: Practical Steps

The vision of APEC Leaders at Seattle was highly practical, building on the lessons of experience, and on their solid and extensive common ground.

The Uruguay Round outcome was a success for APEC Leaders. It is realistic for APEC Leaders now to commit themselves to full and timely implementation of the Round, and to the success of the new WTO. This alone would ensure that the momentum of trade liberalization in APEC economies continues through the remainder of this decade.

APEC Leaders can reasonably commit themselves to going beyond Uruguay Round outcomes, recognizing as they now do that the principal beneficiaries of trade liberalization are the liberalizing economies themselves. APEC leaders and ministers can help to build confidence in each economy that others, too, are opening and so reducing the domestic political costs of unilateral liberalization.

The biggest trade issue over the period ahead in the Asia-Pacific region, as it is in the world economy, is the accommodation of a huge, rapidly growing and liberalizing China. Success will provide strong impetus to trade expansion and economic growth throughout the Asia-Pacific economic community. Early Chinese membership of the WTO, and continued trade reform in China to meet the normal conditions of membership, are necessary conditions for success. It will help if APEC economies are committed to making Chinese entry into the multilateral system work, and to finding solutions to the many problems that will arise along the way. The framework of APEC itself must be consistent with the integration of a reforming and rapidly growing China into the Asia-Pacific economy.

The APEC trade facilitation agenda has large potential for trade expansion. Recognition of its value will help to maintain momentum.

These are all steps towards the building of an Asia-Pacific economic community, that help and not weaken the multilateral institutions, and the economic reform and development efforts in the rest of the world.

APEC leaders could commit themselves to an eventual goal of free trade amongst Asia-Pacific economies in the context of MFN treatment of outsiders. They could agree to report progress towards this goal at each successive meeting of leaders, or, if these are sometimes delayed, of ministers. There would be no threat of sanctions for failure to make progress; just recognition in each country that all gain from continuation of the process, and that progress will cease if most are not seen to be acting upon their commitments. After some time, it may become possible to talk of timetables for achievement of free trade; that can emerge from the process itself. This is the one context — in particular the absence of any threat of sanctions — in which it might be possible to agree on a realistically distant target date. In this context alone, free trade by 2020 might be an acceptable target.

Discussions could commence amongst APEC members of packages of sectoral trade liberalization beyond Uruguay Round commitments, that would be implemented on an MFN basis. Would the free rider problem inhibit progress? Perhaps, on some commodities in some countries. But it is not difficult to identify commodities for which APEC members are overwhelmingly the main suppliers of each others' markets.

Appendix Table 4.1 lists eighty-eight SITC 3-digit commodities for which APEC members supply 75 per cent or more of the region's import requirements, and could be expected to supply the bulk of any expansion of imports following trade liberalization. The list contains many of the commodities in which APEC members' protection against imports is highest, and which are the focus of greatest tension over protection levels: grain and meat, processed wood and metals, subject to tariff escalation, textiles and clothing, toys, motor vehicles, consumer electronics, and telecommunications equipment.

Commodities in which APEC supplies 75 per cent or more of the regional import markets account for almost two thirds of total exports from APEC countries (Appendix Table 4.2). The ratio is lower for economies with high shares of primary exports (Brunei, 38 per cent; Mexico, 44 per cent; and Australia, 50 per cent), but substantial for all and above two-thirds for most.

Presumably, any resentment of free riding would be focussed mainly on Western Europe — the European Union and the former members of European Free Trade (EFTA). One would not expect resentment in large economies at expansion of exports from the liberalizing regions of Indochina, South Asia or Latin America, or from the struggling transitional economies in Eastern Europe or the former Soviet Union, or from poverty-stricken Africa, so strong that it inhibited import liberalization in commodities in which APEC economies supplied more than three quarters of each other's imports. In Appendix Table 4.1, commodities in which total Western European exports to APEC markets are less than 20 per cent of APEC economies' own exports. Even if *schadenfreude* caused APEC economies to forego the gains of trade-liberalization in any commodity in which Western European suppliers were one-fifth as important as APEC, and these commodities were excluded, the remaining "APEC dominated" commodities would represent well over half of total exports from APEC economies (Appendix Table 4.2).

It would, of course, be foolish for APEC economies to allow the free riding problem to inhibit liberalization, even in commodities in which it was likely to be proportionately much larger than in those listed in Appendix Table 4.1. It is a lesson of experience in the Asia-Pacific economic community that the main gains accrue to the liberalizing economy itself. But the data show that even if free riding were a significant inhibition, there would be plenty of scope for liberalization in commodities in which it is likely to be relatively unimportant.

Would liberalization on an MFN basis remove incentives for the European Union (EU) or other economies to enter a new round of multilateral negotiations? Logically, there would be EU interest in expanding liberalization to commodities in which outsiders were proportionately larger suppliers. In any case, it is too heavy a load for APEC to carry, to forego benefits from its own liberalization, in the hope of encouraging progress in a new round of multilateral negotiations. Objectives in the multilateral system are secured more appropriately through multilateral institutions — in this case, through strong APEC support, and action through, the new WTO. It is stretching belief to assert that the WTO would be strengthened through a major part of its membership breaking its rules, as would be the case with any real-world full or partial PAFTA.

Sectoral trade liberalization is consistent with the multilateral rules only on an MFN basis. And negotiated trade liberalization by sub-sets of a regional group, the 18 minus X, is consistent with maintenance of support for the multilateral system, on an MFN basis only.

The proposed course has the potential for accelerating progress towards free trade in the region. But if, in practice, it delivered disappointing outcomes, it would do no harm — to established processes of trade liberalization, to APEC as an institution with its potential for good in other areas, to the standing of regional leaders, to political relations among APEC states, to the prospects for reform and growth in neighbouring countries, or to the multilateral trading system in the aftermath of the Uruguay Round. In this it would be unlike unsuccessful attempts to establish a traditional free trade area — with the requirement to announce timetables, and with the invitation to tit for tat behaviour inherent in discrimination against outsiders and against APEC members that failed to meet the lists.

V APEC: A Practical Agenda

The next meeting of APEC leaders in Bogor, Indonesia, in November 1994, will have an opportunity to build on the solid foundations laid in Seattle and at ministerial and official meetings before and since. There is much good to be done, without drifting into fantasy, or into risky territory.

Continuation and extension of the progress on trade and investment facilitation should be recognized as enhancing in a major way the benefits from APEC. And despite the controversy over the precise meaning of free trade, there is much that can be done on trade liberalization. If discriminatory free trade were removed from the agenda, the productive elements of the Seattle vision could be taken much further. I would suggest an unequivocal commitment to eventual free trade, and to steady progress towards that eventual goal. And, if they chose, APEC leaders could, consistent with their secure common ground, agree to go further, into an attempt to accelerate trade liberalization through sectoral negotiations on commodities at least in which APEC economies dominate exports to each others' markets.

The APEC leaders meeting will also provide a favourable forum for raising the importance of development co-operation in the APEC agenda, with a view to APEC economies working explicitly towards the strengthening of the weak spots in regional prosperity and growth.

APPENDIX TABLE 4.1

Commodities (SITC 3-Digit) in which Imports from APEC Countries Dominate Total APEC Imports, 1992

(APEC Share Exceeds 75%)

SITC Code	Commodity Description	Imports from APEC as Share of Total APEC Imports %	Value of APEC Imports from APEC Countries US$ billions	Value of APEC Imports from Western Europe (EFTA plus EEC 12) US$ billions
351	Electric Energy	100	1.0	0.0*
046	Wheat etc Meal or Flour	99	0.2	0.0*
241	Fuel Wood and Charcoal	96	0.1	0.0*
274	Sulphur etc	96	0.3	0.0*
243	Wood Shaped	96	9.2	0.0*
044	Maize Unmilled	96	4.1	0.0*
043	Barley Unmilled	95	0.4	0.0*
001	Live Animals	95	2.6	0.1*
631	Veneers, Plywood, etc	95	6.2	0.1*
891	Sound Recorders, Producers	94	23.1	1.4*
733	Road Vehicles Non-Motor	92	4.0	0.2*
422	Fixed veg oil nonsoft	92	1.5	0.0*
091	Margarine, Shortening	92	0.1	0.0*
041	Wheat etc Unmilled	91	4.2	0.1*
685	Lead	91	0.4	0.0*
032	Fish etc Tinned, Prepared	91	2.8	0.1*
714	Office Machines	91	62.5	5.5*
894	Toys, Sporting Goods, etc	90	19.3	1.6*
321	Coal, Coke, Briquettes	90	9.1	0.0*
724	Telecommunications Equip	90	45.3	4.2*
047	Meal and Flour Non-Wheat	89	0.1	0.0*
723	Electr Distributing Mach	89	7.3	0.8*
729	Electrical Machinery Nes	88	73.3	8.6*
431	Processed Animal Veg Oil, etc	87	0.7	0.1*
242	Wood Rough	87	5.6	0.0*
632	Wood Manufactures Nes	87	2.5	0.3*
221	Oil Seeds, Nuts, Kernals	87	3.9	0.1*
251	Pulp and Waste Paper	87	6.2	0.3*
231	Rubber Crude, Synthetic	86	3.7	0.4*
011	Meat Fresh, Chilled, Frozen	86	10.1	1.1*
893	Articles of Plastic Nes	85	10.1	1.6*
653	Woven Textiles Noncotton	85	17.1	2.3*
211	Hides, Skins, Undressed	85	2.0	0.3*

SITC Code	Commodity Description	Imports from APEC as Share of Total APEC Imports %	Value of APEC Imports from APEC Countries US$ billions	Value of APEC Imports from Western Europe (EFTA plus EEC 12) US$ billions
863	Developed Cinema Film	85	0.2	0.0*
694	Steel, Copper Nails, etc	85	2.7	0.4*
899	Other Manufactured Goods	85	6.6	1.1*
267	Waste of Textile Fabrics	84	0.2	0.0*
054	Veg etc Frsh, Smply Prsvd	84	3.8	0.3*
411	Animal Oils and Fats	84	0.3	0.0*
725	Domestic Electric Equip	84	7.4	1.2*
642	Articles of Paper etc	84	3.3	0.6*
664	Glass	83	3.1	0.6*
286	Uranium, Thorium Ore, Conc	83	0.3	0.0*
266	Synthetic, Regenrtd Fibre	83	2.0	0.3*
732	Road Motor Vehicles	83	114.2	22.3*
262	Wool and Animal Hair	83	2.3	0.2*
282	Iron and Steel Scrap	82	1.4	0.2*
042	Rice	82	0.7	0.0*
812	Plumbg, Heating, Lghtng Equ	81	3.0	0.6*
654	Lace, Ribbons, Tulle, etc	81	1.1	0.2*
045	Cereals Nes Unmilled	81	1.0	0.1*
025	Eggs	81	0.3	0.0*
099	Food Preparations Nes	81	2.2	0.4*
291	Crude Animal Matter Nes	81	1.2	0.1*
621	Materials of Rubber	80	1.1	0.3
581	Plastic Materials etc	80	19.8	4.2
687	Tin	80	0.6	0.0*
722	Elec Pwr Mach, Switchgear	80	27.7	6.4
697	Base Mtl Household Equip	79	2.1	0.4*
261	Silk	79	0.3	0.0*
821	Furniture	79	9.1	2.1
698	Metal Manufactures Nes	79	7.5	1.8*
652	Cotton Fabrics, Woven	79	5.6	0.5*
655	Special Textile etc Prod	79	4.0	0.9*
842	Fur etc Clothes, Prod	78	0.4	0.1*
122	Tobacco Mfrs	78	4.3	1.1
682	Copper	78	6.6	0.7*
641	Paper and Paperboard	78	13.4	3.5
571	Explosives, Pyrotech Prod	78	0.6	0.1
521	Coal, Petroleum etc Chems	78	0.6	0.1*
851	Footwear	77	13.5	2.2*
656	Textile etc Products Nes	78	2.6	0.3*
055	Vegtbles etc Prsvd, Prepd	78	1.6	0.4

SITC Code	Commodity Description	Imports from APEC as Share of Total APEC Imports %	Value of APEC Imports from APEC Countries US$ billions	Value of APEC Imports from Western Europe (EFTA plus EEC 12) US$ billions
081	Animal Feeding Stuff	77	3.8	0.3*
674	Irn, Stl Univ, Plate, Sheet	77	11.6	2.3*
831	Travel Goods, Handbags	77	6.0	1.6
895	Office Supplies Nes	77	1.7	0.5
111	Non-Alc Beverages Nes	77	0.7	0.2
678	Iron, Stl Tubes, Pipes, etc	77	4.6	1.1
341	Gas Natural and Manufctd	77	12.4	0.1*
686	Zinc	76	1.4	0.2*
283	Nonfer Base Mtl Ore, Conc	76	4.9	0.1*
554	Soaps, Cleaning etc Preps	76	1.4	0.4
692	Metal Tanks, Boxes, etc	76	1.0	0.2
841	Clothing Not of Fur	76	46.5	4.4*
285	Silver and Platinum Ores	75	0.2	0.1
861	Instruments, Apparatus	75	24.6	7.4
276	Other Crude Minerals	75	2.0	0.2

* Indicates Western European exports to APEC markets equal 20 per cent or less of APEC exports to APEC markets.

Source: The Australian National University, International Economic Databank.

APPENDIX TABLE 4.2

APEC Countries: Value of APEC Exports in Commodities in which APEC Suppliers Dominate APEC Imports, 1992

Exporting Country	APEC-dominated Commodities		*Schadenfreude*-modified APEC-dominated Commodities	
	Value of APEC Economies' Exports of Commodities in which APEC Supplies in Excess of 75% of APEC Imports		Exports of APEC Countries of APEC-Dominated Export Commodities in which Western Europe Supplies Less Than One Fifth as much as APEC Exporters to APEC Markets	
	US$ billions	Percent of Exporting Country's Total Exports	US$ billions	Percent of Country's Total Exports
Australia	19.1	50	18.1	48
Brunei	1.0	38	1.0	38
Canada	89.0	68	73.6	56
Chile	6.7	70	6.4	67
China	101.8	80	88.4	69
Hong Kong	24.3	80	20.7	68
Indonesia	22.5	67	21.0	62
Japan	235.4	69	193.8	57
Korea, Rep	54.0	71	46.1	61
Mexico	11.9	44	10.2	38
Malaysia	33.6	80	30.7	73
New Zealand	4.9	52	4.3	46
Philippines	5.1	52	4.5	46
Papua New Guinea	0.8	77	0.8	76
Singapore	41.5	65	35.4	56
Thailand	19.6	68	17.5	61
Taiwan	62.4	80	49.3	63
USA	232.3	55	180.0	43
APEC Total	965.9	65.7	802.0	54.5

Source: The Australian National University, International Economic Databank.

5
THE BOGOR DECLARATION ON ASIA-PACIFIC TRADE LIBERALIZATION

History seems to move slowly in East Asia. What was for a while called the "East Asian Miracle" crept up on an unsuspecting world. There was no storming of the Bastille; no Gettysburg address; no pulling down of the Berlin Wall.

That is not to forget the drama in this city almost three decades ago, that marked the rise to power of tomorrow's host in Bogor. But even in the birth of the New Order in Jakarta, who in the West, or in Indonesia, foreshadowed then, or a decade later, the emergence of the dynamic, internationally-oriented industrializing economy that we see around us?

The "East Asian Miracle" has been marked by gradualism and consistency of purpose over long periods. Enough policy change is introduced to get a new pattern of economic growth under way; and more steps are taken to remove barriers to growth

---

This chapter was first presented at a conference organized by the Centre for Strategic and International Studies in Jakarta on the eve of the Bogor Summit in November 1994. It is reproduced with the permission of the Centre for Strategic and International Studies.

as they are identified. Trade liberalization plays a part in making a start and keeping it going. No single step to shake the *New York Times* or the *Sydney Morning Herald*. Who made much of each step in China's trade liberalization, taken for its own reasons and mostly at its own pace, and adding US$40 billion per annum to the exports of its partners around the world? But we look up after a while, and the structure of global trade and economic power has been transformed.

On the scale of single steps in the history of internationally-oriented growth in East Asia, the Bogor meeting of APEC Leaders is shaping up to be rather big. For people who judge history by the grander standards of Congressional landslides, there will be disappointment. Who will wake up the day after the Summit and be sure that anything has changed?

Neither APEC nor its leaders' meetings created the Asia-Pacific community. That has been built brick by brick by millions of hands over these last several decades — American and East Asian and Australasian hands together. I expect, nevertheless, that when we look back not from Wednesday morning but from some years hence, the events in Bogor will have helped to lift the Asia-Pacific community to new heights of achievement.

It is already a secure achievement of the Bogor meeting that the importance of Indonesia in the practical affairs of our region is more widely understood. It is already a secure achievement of Bogor that in a year that began with severe and disruptive tensions in trans-Pacific relations, the United States has put the effort into relations with Japan, China and the ASEAN states to provide an appropriate place for the issues that bind the Asia-Pacific community. It is already a secure achievement of these days on Java, that the development of the Asia-Pacific's poorer member economies is part of the agenda of official and collective concern. It is already a secure achievement that the established agenda of trade and investment facilitation in our region — measures to reduce the costs of transactions across our borders — has been given additional depth and momentum.

These are large achievements, before I get to trade liberalization. They might turn out to be the main achievements, however successful the discussion of trade liberalization at the Summit.

The Best Possible Outcome

The leaders' statement may contain the following on trade liberalization

(a)   a commitment to liberalization towards free and open trade in the region
(b)   a target date for achieving free and open trade in the region
(c)   a requirement of consistency with GATT/WTO rules and principles
(d)   details to be worked out by APEC Ministers.
I will call this the "Indonesian formula".

There will probably be a different pace for different countries, but maybe not enough thought has been given to how hard it would actually be to implement genuinely free trade in the United States by 2010.

Note the words "liberalization towards free and open trade in the region" rather than "free trade". An alternative formulation of equivalent effect would talk about "aims" and "targets". Some leaders would want to say that the agreement is "non-binding"; others would say that the non-binding character of APEC's decisions are implicit in the APEC process as it has evolved over these past five years.

It is still possible that leaders could pull back from these words, as they did at Seattle, because of lack of clarity about what is meant to be the content of "free trade". There is no need for them to do so. Read carefully, the words say enough to meet the requirements of those who have greatest caution.

These words say some definite things. They establish a new goal of free trade in each country's relations with each other APEC member. It is a big step for Japan, Korea and Taiwan to announce a goal of free trade in agriculture. It is something new for the United States to commit itself to move towards free trade with China: it has not, till now, committed itself even to treating Chinese imports on the same basis as other economies outside NAFTA. In China, the debate about liberalizing agricultural trade has barely begun as domestic demand drives domestic grain prices well above world prices in emulation of its Northeast Asian neighbours. In liberalizing Australia, protectionist interests in the car and clothing industries have been put on notice that genuine free trade is back on the agenda after a few years' reprieve.

These would be stronger commitments to the objective of free trade than have ever been made by the contracting parties to the GATT, or the G7. They would represent a major shift in the Asia-Pacific landscape on protection and trade liberalization. And remember that these are serious leaders, who need to take each other seriously. Otherwise it would have been rather easier to reach a "non-binding agreement".

Words about GATT rules or principles will have significance. They mean most-favoured-nation treatment of all GATT contracting partners unless trade discrimination is allowed under Article 24 of the GATT. Amongst other requirements of Article 24, to justify discrimination in favour of APEC members under the GATT there would need to be a binding agreement to establish free trade in substantially all products between all members of APEC, and a plan and schedule of transition to free trade. The Uruguay Round has hardened the requirements: the transitional period must be no longer than ten years.

Elsewhere the requirements of Article 24 have been honoured more in the breach than the observance. Explicit mention of the GATT/WTO rules will mean that in this case the rules are meant to be observed. It is important that they are. It has been recognized for some time that Article 24 requires shoring up, lest the central pillar of the GATT, Article 1, "the-most-favoured-nation" provision, be undermined. For such a major group of trading nations as the APEC members to fail to observe the WTO principles would be to weaken fatally the new trade body from its inception.

The Indonesian formula in itself would not justify discrimination under Article 24, nor launch a negotiation amongst APEC members to develop a binding schedule of reductions in protection to produce free trade that might one day qualify under Article 24.

There may be additional signals in the words of the Indonesian formula to exclude this possibility. "Open" trade once had a precise meaning within APEC: free trade between members without discrimination against outsiders. There have been recent attempts to give it different meanings, most notably in the second (but not the first) report of the Eminent Persons Group. I have no doubt that, if the word "open" appears, the original meaning will have been intended by the hosts who are proposing it, that it will have been read that way in at least several East Asian countries, and that attempts to redefine it would be seen as a breach of faith. The protracted transition to free trade would be inconsistent with any attempt to initiate APEC free trade under Article 24 — the more so if some APEC members intend to press ahead early with trade liberalization.

After the prominence given to the free trade objective over the past year, it would be a large blow to progress in APEC if there were no agreement at Bogor. It would, of course, be better to have no agreement, than an agreement designed to look good at a single meeting, and which lived on only as a reminder that in 1994 APEC leaders announced something beyond their capacity to deliver. But given the reality of Asia-Pacific trade expansion and liberalization over the past decade, the Indonesian formula represents a realistic ambition, and a basis for realistic progress.

There will be scepticism about an agreement which at least some say is "not binding".

However, the process of trade liberalization in some sectors of our economies is so recent, the path ahead so uncertain, and the immediate political constraints so pressing that credibility requires some caution at least about the timing of free trade end points. Stronger words might be used, but not credibly. The United States government has taken large, constructive steps to improve the environment for expansion of trans-Pacific economic relations this year; but who could predict the outcome of a decision to seek Congressional approval to reduce barriers to zero in its trade with Japan or China? Caution in the phrasing of the agreement will reflect prudent and responsible leadership.

Some will be disappointed that the Indonesian formula does not provide the basis for discriminatory trade under Article 24. The reality is that this was not desirable and there was never any prospect of reaching agreement of this kind. While some elements in the United States polity are attracted by the kind of reciprocity implicit in discriminatory trade, the Congress has placed explicit and implicit conditions on entry into new free trade agreements. One is the linkage of such agreements to labour and environmental issues — a linkage explicitly repudiated by the ASEAN states. The political problems of firm commitment to free trade with Japan and China are greater still. Japan, at least, has firm and principled objections to entry into discriminatory blocs that would preclude going down that path.

For the institution of APEC itself, caution along the lines of the Indonesian formula is a prudent reflection of reality. APEC was built on the understanding that progress would be gradual, by consensus, and by informal rather than binding agreements.

This was the explicit basis of ASEAN participation in APEC from the early days. To change abruptly on issues of fundamental importance to every member economy would corrode the basis of all the progress that has been made within APEC.

A Good Outcome

The Indonesian formula provides a good basis for setting out immediately to develop a worthwhile programme of most-favoured-nation trade liberalization, and none for proceeding with discriminatory liberalization. These are two large virtues. Non-discriminatory liberalization has the following advantages for APEC.

- It provides no discouragement to maintaining the momentum in productive trade liberalization in the Western Pacific, no encouragement to hold back "concessions" as coin in negotiations on an APEC trade liberalization timetable.
- It avoids the possibility of APEC-sponsored trade liberalization leading to new discrimination in the treatment of APEC members by each other — a development that would quickly corrode support for APEC.
- It does not place new barriers in the path of internationally-oriented reform in developing and transitional economies that remain outside APEC, including Vietnam, India and Russia. (It would certainly be a discouragement if these economies were required to compete on less favourable terms than China and Indonesia in the United States market.)
- It avoids new rules of origin associated with APEC trade liberalization which, if they were made necessary, would inhibit greatly finer specialization and expanded intra-industry trade which are becoming more important within the region.
- It encourages an immediate start on APEC trade liberalization without negotiation of a liberalization schedule covering

substantially all trade, ratification through the various national processes and presentation to the WTO.

- It encourages some countries to move before others are able to make formal and binding commitments on free trade.
- It encourages countries that are not able to secure legislative approval now for a programme that qualifies under Article 24, to make a start in areas where the political constraints are less tight.
- It allows sectoral agreements in advance of binding commitments to comprehensive liberalization.
- Most importantly of all, it ensures APEC trade liberalization will be GATT-consistent in spirit, in practice and in law. APEC will be positioned to lead the next major round of global negotiations through the WTO when the time is right.

If, as I believe to be the case, the Indonesian formula precludes APEC-sponsored trade discrimination, there would have been some advantages in saying so. In particular, more explicit statements on this point would have avoided the possibility that one or more APEC members fail to get the message, and rather than getting on with the job of moving towards free trade the region, spends the year leading to Osaka, as it did in the path to Seattle last year, and now Bogor, debating the character of APEC free trade. Clearer statements would have made it quite clear that Bogor, unlike Seattle, had not postponed the free trade decision. But let us hope that the Indonesian formula as it is ends the debate.

Some argue that discriminatory liberalization would provide stronger incentives for outsiders, notably the European Union, to enter a new round of multilateral negotiations. This is not an important advantage in practice over the Indonesian formula: APEC can proceed as far as possible with non-discriminatory liberalization in the period immediately ahead, and then offer to complete the movement to free trade in the context of a global negotiation under the auspices of the WTO. It is not at all clear that such a process would be less effective in launching a new round than the distant threat of direct confrontation of Europe by the formation of a free trade area. Proud though we may be of the progress that APEC has made, it would be naive to think that its internal cohesion and solidarity would yet sustain a highly combative approach to trade relations with the rest of the world.

Some might also argue that an advantage of discriminatory trade is that, at least at first blush, it is more attractive to the United States polity. The potential advantage in practice may not be real. The reality is that there is no prospect of a formal, binding APEC free trade area that can meet the tests of Article 24, and in a form that is acceptable in East Asia, passing muster in the United States Congress for the foreseeable future. It must nevertheless be acknowledged that it will be a major challenge for other APEC members to attract the participation of the United States in meaningful non-discriminatory liberalization.

Is the Indonesian formula good enough actually to make a difference? "What is the value", critics will say, "of belonging to a club that confers no favours to members over non-members"?

The Indonesian formula would help real trade liberalization in two ways.

First, while each country benefits from its own liberalization whatever other countries do, it benefits more if others are liberalizing as well. If each government is confident that its neighbours are liberalizing, the cost-benefit calculations, taking into account the costs of adjustment, are more strongly favourable for liberalization.

The second way that it would help is through changing perceptions of trade policy behaviour in partner economies. Popular or even governmental perceptions that others are free riding becomes a justification for holding back on one's own liberalization. By agreeing to liberalize together and, even more importantly, by doing so and demonstrating that they are doing so, APEC members can ease the political economy constraints on each of their trade liberalization.

The Path Forward

The remarkable growth and structural transformation of Asia-Pacific economies over the past generation have been underwritten by the combination of access to markets abroad and trade liberalization at home. Over the past decade, growth, trade liberalization, structural change and import growth in East Asia have provided the largest part of export market growth for East Asia itself, taking over North America's old role (Figures 5.1 and 5.4). At the same time, East Asia has become the most rapidly growing market for North American exports, although intra-North American exports, now to be spurred by NAFTA, remain absolutely larger (Figures 5.2 and 5.5). East Asia, mainly, and the Western Pacific as a whole, have contributed virtually the whole of the growth of exports from Oceania (Australia, Papua New Guinea, New Zealand) since 1985 (Figures 5.3 and 5.6).

The import expansion flowing from dynamism and trade liberalization of East Asia has enhanced export performance throughout the Asia-Pacific region. This has more than compensated for sluggish growth in East Asian and Oceanian exports to North America. The fact that North American exports have been rising faster than imports from East Asia since the mid-1980s has taken the edge off tensions that arose in the period of the strong dollar in the first half of the 1980s, when East Asian export growth was strongly focused on the United States.

These tendencies are all highly favourable for growth, and for deepening Asia-Pacific economic co-operation. There is no need in the Asia-Pacific to reverse old and unfavourable tendencies in trade policy and trends, as there may be in Europe, Latin America and Europe. Economic integration across borders within the Asia-

FIGURE 5.1

**East Asia: Volume of Merchandise Exports by
Destination, 1985–93** (1985=100)

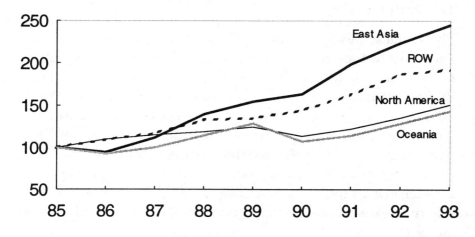

FIGURE 5.2

**North America: Volume of Merchandise Exports by
Destination, 1985–93** (1985=100)

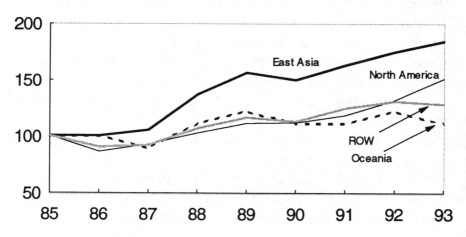

FIGURE 5.3

Oceania: Volume of Merchandise Exports by Destination, 1985–93 (1985=100)

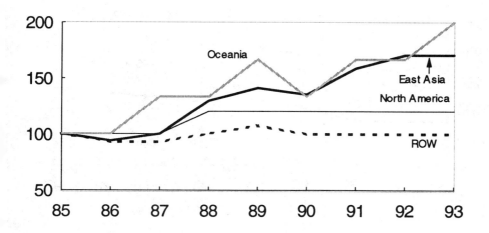

FIGURE 5.4

East Asia: Merchandise Exports in Constant 1993 Prices, by Destination, 1985–93 (US$ billions)

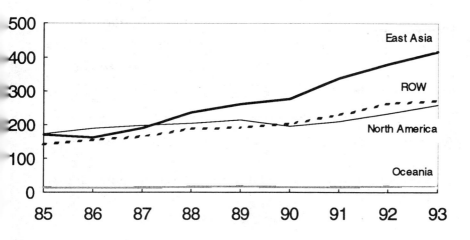

FIGURE 5.5

North America: Merchandise Exports in Constant 1993 Prices, by Destination, 1985–93 (US$ billions)

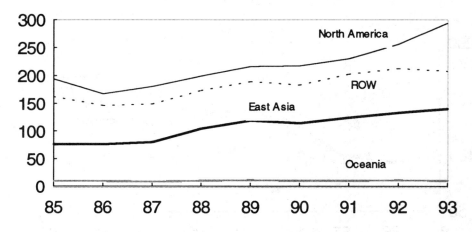

FIGURE 5.6

Oceania: Merchandise Exports in Constant 1993 Prices, by Destination, 1985–93 (US$ billions)

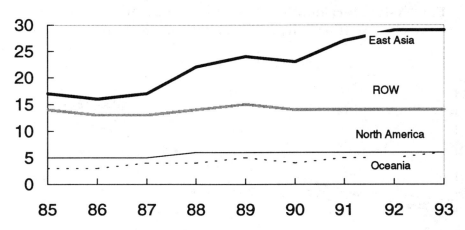

Source: International Economic Databank, ANU, Canberra for all the above Figures 5.1 to 5.6.

Pacific has been proceeding rapidly under the combined influences of market forces and, within each country, trade liberalization and market-oriented reform. The region will do well if these healthy, well-established tendencies can be sustained. The task of intergovernmental co-operation within APEC is a conservative one: to do what it can to preserve these favourable trends.

Will a decision along the lines of the Indonesian formula help to maintain these favourable tendencies in Asia-Pacific trade expansion?

It is important to remember that decisions on the reduction of trade barriers at the border are taken in individual APEC member economies, although influenced to some extent by international pressures and opportunities. Remembering this, the question is: will agreement under the Indonesian formula help the political economy of trade liberalization in each economy? I think so. At least, there is no danger of such a decision establishing cross-currents that threaten established trends.

Unilateral liberalization is still proceeding apace in many Western Pacific countries, notably Malaysia and Australia. Indonesia is responding with deregulation to competition for investment from China and India. Business-driven deregulation and institutional change in Japan is interacting with the high yen to expand the importance of earlier reductions of manufacturing protection. Chinese reform is proceeding as rapidly over the past year as at any time in the reform era, and may soon, hopefully very soon, be joined by implementation of far-reaching commitments to reduce protection upon entry into the WTO. Taiwan has less to offer on entry to the WTO because it has liberalized more already, but its entry will nevertheless be accompanied by substantial further reductions in protection. Uruguay Round-related undertakings are bringing highly protected agricultural activity within the international rules for the first time in Japan, Taiwan and Korea. Chile and Mexico are well into important programmes of internationally-oriented reform. And the whole region, its various members in varying degrees, will soon, a Republican Congress willing in the United States, be engaged in reducing protection in line with Uruguay Round commitments. For the Asia-Pacific, the United States' Uruguay Round commitments are particularly significant where they will remove the quantitative restrictions and main "grey area" measures (especially the Multifibre Arrangement) that have accumulated over two decades and compromised what had been an economy very open to foreign trade.

Asia-Pacific economies can move towards the implementation of the ambitious goals that will be set in Bogor through

- the pressing ahead with unilateral liberalization in the region alongside the faithful implementation on the Uruguay Round
- the exploration of opportunities for additional progress in sectors of special importance to APEC countries
- supporting the initiation by APEC of a new global negotiation when the opportunity is ripe towards the end of the century.

The alternative would be a long negotiation to determine whether trade discrimination under Article 24 is consistent with the Bogor Declaration, leading to a binding, hard, free trade decision at another leaders' meeting; and then a long negotiation of schedules for liberalization to free trade over a ten-year period, presumably between 2000 and 2010 for developed countries; and then a battle for approval of a comprehensive free trade agreement through each of our governmental processes, including a United States Congress that has recently in effect refused the Administration fast-track authority on new trade agreements.

To harness the tide of on-going Asia-Pacific liberalization of the mid-1990s to implementation of the Bogor Declaration, there are three initial requirements.

The first is acceptance within APEC that the Bogor Declaration defines the parameters of APEC trade liberalization for the foreseeable future — for long enough to learn what can be made of it. This means acceptance of the non-binding commitments, aims rather than enforceable commitments, and by implication liberalization under the most-favoured-nation provision of the WTO. There is no need to decide that this will never change; that developments within APEC and in the rest of the world would not change the relative value of, and constraints on, various approaches.

A second requirement is the development of a mechanism that can monitor the extent of protection in each member country independently, authoritatively and professionally. With the decisions of each country determining the rate at which it approaches free trade, there will be much scope for misperception and dispute about whether each country is doing enough. There will be no penalties for breach of non-binding agreements. Enforcement will depend on domestic and international public review and peer pressure at all levels of government. It will depend, too, on each government realizing that the implementation of non-binding commitments that together are of great value to it, depend on every country including its own pulling its weight; and realizing that otherwise others will become disillusioned with the process and withdraw.

Objective and authoritative measurement and publication of results will bring all progress in APEC trade liberalization to account in forming perceptions about whether others are doing their share. This is especially important in informing the United States polity on trans-Pacific developments.

There are various ways in which measurement could be managed. It would be easiest politically to rely on national institutions in each country; but this may not be seen to meet the requirement on independence. Another possibility is that the Disputes Settlement

Mechanism recommended in the second Eminent Persons Group report, with its expert panels, could have its responsibilities broadened to include the monitoring of protection and changes in its level over time. It would report annually to APEC Ministers and subsequently publish its findings. Let us call this informal institution the "Trade Liberalization Panel" when serving this purpose.

The third requirement is already present within APEC — acceptance that APEC trade liberalization is built upon and designed to strengthen and to extend, the role of the WTO and the new international rules. It is important in this context that APEC economies support the entry of China and Taiwan into the WTO, that they are committed to full and timely implementation of the Uruguay Round and to making the WTO's new mechanisms work; and to acting consistently within the new rules.

The challenge for APEC members would be to use the Bogor Declaration to maintain pressure for trade liberalization at a rate that, if maintained, would at least meet the free trade target dates. In the period immediately ahead, perhaps through to the late 1990s, the implementation of on-going domestic reforms, the Uruguay Round, and in China and Taiwan the WTO entry commitments, are likely to maintain progress at a rate which, if maintained until 2010 or 2020, would achieve the goals of the Bogor Declaration. The challenge is now to develop the approaches that will sustain this rate of liberalization beyond these early years. The maintenance of momentum in the Western Pacific's largest communities, in which there is a long way to go, China and Indonesia, will not be an easy matter. The framework provided by the Bogor Declaration, if given real substance through substantive actions by APEC members, would significantly improve the chances of success in China and Indonesia.

Western Pacific economies will need to recognize the special circumstances of the United States. The United States has accepted in the Uruguay Round large burdens of adjustment which will be of great value to East Asia and Australasia. This will keep liberalization in the United States proceeding until the end of the century at a rate that would, if maintained lead to free trade in the United States by 2010. This would leave the United States a very open economy at the end of the century. The adjustment costs of these changes in the United States will be considerable, and the United States polity is not altogether reconciled to them. For all of these reasons, it is neither necessary nor realistic for other APEC members to ask for more trade liberalization from the United States over the next few years than has been committed in the Uruguay Round. Hopefully, the constraints on United States' contributions to APEC liberalization will gradually be loosened as the reality of far-reaching liberalization in the Western Pacific comes to be recognized more clearly in the United States, helped by the publicity on Asia-Pacific trade and economic progress that is associated with high-level United States participation in APEC Leaders' meetings.

Continued progress within the framework of the Bogor Declaration must be based on continued progress in trade liberalization in APEC members other than the United States. Such progress will require efforts in the wide range of activities that are consistent with non-discriminatory reductions in protection, unilaterally, regionally and globally through the WTO.

- It is desirable for APEC members to agree on a protection standstill to support the Bogor Declaration. This is of substantial importance, because in many APEC members, notably the ASEAN countries, protection levels are already well below those bound in the Uruguay Round.
- Each APEC member could take one substantial step in reductions in protection by the time of the next APEC meeting in Osaka.
- It is desirable for some members of APEC to accept the roles of trade liberalization locomotives, going well beyond the Uruguay

Round commitments and the Bogor Declaration critical path in the early years. One of these members must be Japan. Japan has exercised considerable leadership within APEC over the past year in insisting on non-discriminatory liberalization; it has shown that it can say no to bad ideas. It is now necessary for it to say yes to good ideas; and to exercise leadership in the preparations for the Osaka summit.

- There is wide scope for progress on trade liberalization in identified sectors on a most-favoured-nation basis. There is no need for every APEC economy to participate in a decision to liberalize in each specified sector. A country that is concerned to avoid free-riding by others, especially Europeans, could choose to enter sectoral agreements only in commodities in which European countries have little competitive strength in Asia-Pacific markets. Alternatively, APEC could prepare sectoral liberalization agreements for negotiation globally through the WTO. There are opportunities to sculpt packages of sectoral liberalizing agreements, across which it is possible to balance opportunities for participating members to expand exports.
- Every chance can be taken to engage the rest of the world in discussions of liberalization within the new structures of the WTO.
- Most importantly of all, each member must recognize that it is crucial for it to maintain liberalization at a rate that, if maintained, would reach the Bogor Declaration goals, and would be going faster still at times and in sectors where there is domestic political opportunity.

We cannot be certain that these efforts to maintain momentum in implementation of the Bogor Declaration will be decisive in maintaining the Asia-Pacific trade expansion of recent times. But they should help. They will be most powerful if they, and their reflection in the reports of the Trade Liberalization Panel, begin to reduce the United States' sense of grievance about trans-Pacific trade relations.

If it all works, the success of the Bogor Declaration will be reflected in the continuation of Asia-Pacific trade expansion and opportunity for prosperity. The biggest achievement will have been to ease and to secure the integration into the Asia-Pacific and world economies of those members who, like China and Indonesia, are committed to internationalization, but who are as yet at an early stage in the journey.

By late in the decade, APEC members will be in a strong position to engage the rest of the world in discussion of major new steps in trade liberalization within the WTO. This would be productive reciprocity that avoids the many pitfalls of discriminatory trade in a large region.

6

THE WESTERN PACIFIC PARADIGM AND THE SINGAPORE MINISTERIAL MEETING OF THE WTO

History sometimes confers on an event a significance beyond the initial expectations of its organizers and participants.

The new World Trade Organization and the Trade Ministers certainly expect important outcomes from the WTO Ministerial Meeting in Singapore in November.

It is the first Ministerial Meeting of the WTO.

It is the time when progress in implementing the Uruguay Round commitments is subjected to high-level review.

It is the time when members take stock on the future programme of trade negotiations built into the Uruguay Round decisions.

It is the time when members distil the conclusions of the many less or more formal meetings of WTO members since Marrakesh on new trade negotiations. If there is broad support for a comprehensive new round of multilateral negotiations, ministers will discuss its scope, ambition and modus operandus. If there is

This chapter was first presented to the World Trade Congress in Singapore in April 1996. It is reproduced with the permission of the Singapore Trade Development Board.

not, then they will discuss the time at which it would be appropriate to raise the matter again, or the alternative means of keeping multilateral trade liberalization moving.

These are no small matters.

But the Singapore meeting is more important still.

A Western Pacific Paradigm

The Singapore meeting will be the occasion in history when a new paradigm, a Western Pacific paradigm, may become an important organizing idea of the multilateral trading system and the World Trade Organization.

The new paradigm has emerged from discussion and experience in the most rapidly expanding, the most rapidly liberalizing (although not the most liberal) and now the largest regional centre of world trade expansion — the Western Pacific region extending through Northeast Asia, Southeast Asia and the Southwest Pacific (Tables 6.1 and 6.2).

The Western Pacific paradigm is that of concerted unilateral liberalization, directed to an ultimate goal of multilateral free trade, based on voluntary and non-binding commitments, and enforced by peer pressure, recognition that all must participate if the beneficent process is to succeed, and most fundamentally by recognition that each country's liberalization is in the interest of development in the liberalizing economy itself.

The new paradigm has become the organizing idea of the world's most ambitious exercise in regional trade liberalization, through Asia-Pacific Economic Co-operation.

The new paradigm has the potential to carry the multilateral trading system forward at a time when progress has become difficult within the old paradigm. The old paradigm was embodied in the General Agreement on Tariffs and Trade, the GATT. The GATT paradigm was based on reciprocal reductions in protection, in

TABLE 6.1

Real Increment in World Imports, 1985–94

(US$ billions)

	From World	From West Pacific APEC	From East Pacific APEC	From EU-12	From Rest of the World
World	1656	644	319	571	122
Japan	102	49	32	23	−2
Developing Northeast Asian countries	345	222	50	45	28
Developing Southeast Asian countries	186	114	28	25	19
Oceania	25	12	6	4	2
West Pacific APEC	322	122	140	29	30
East Pacific APEC	658	397	117	97	47
APEC	980	519	257	127	78
EU-12	564	99	43	338	84
Rest of world	112	34	19	107	−47

Note: Nominal value of imports is deflated by GATT/WTO unit value index for exports (1990=100).

Source: UN trade data, International Economic Databank, Australian National University.

TABLE 6.2
World Imports, 1994
(US$ billions)

	From World	From West Pacific APEC	From East Pacific APEC	From EU-12	From Rest of the World
World	4194	1181	778	1424	810
Japan	272	107	76	35	55
Developing Northeast Asian countries	453	277	71	56	48
Developing Southeast Asian countries	272	160	43	36	33
Oceania	65	29	15	13	7
West Pacific APEC	1062	574	205	141	142
East Pacific APEC	926	313	346	138	128
APEC	1987	887	551	279	271
EU-12	1444	164	129	803	348
Rest of world	763	138	98	342	184

Note: Nominal value of imports is deflated by GATT/WTO unit value index for exports (1990=100).
Source: UN trade data, International Economic Databank, Australian National University.

which each country's liberalization was seen as a "concession" benefiting other countries and as a price for securing liberalization in others. Reciprocal bargains were enforced by penalties for breaches of binding commitments, and ultimately by the power of the United States to withdraw some of the considerable favour and support that was once within its capacity to confer.

The GATT paradigm reflected the ideas that held sway in the political economy of the country that, at GATT's inception and through its early decades, dominated international trade and investment: the United States.

The GATT paradigm replaced the international economic anarchy, the "beggar thy neighbour" protectionism and currency depreciation of the 1930s. It was brilliantly successful in providing stability in trade relations and securing substantially open trade amongst the major industrial economies of the Northern Hemisphere. It had its weaknesses: the exclusion of the GATT principles from agricultural and textiles trade; the exclusion of the large part of the world that was on the communist side of the Cold War; the effective exemption of developing countries from the trade policy disciplines through the provision for special and differential treatment; the difficulty of managing trade distortions resulting from policy interventions (like subsidies) that were not imposed at the border. As market pressures led to deeper and more intimate economic integration across national frontiers, issues not yet covered by GATT disciplines came to be seen as proper subjects for international negotiations and agreement, including issues of investment and intellectual property rights that had trade implications. A new climate of support for regional trade arrangements increased the importance of strengthening the rules for regional free trade arrangements under Article 24 of GATT.

But for all these weaknesses, GATT provided an important part of the framework first for rapid post-war reconstruction in

Europe and Japan, and then for the emergence of what has been called inaccurately the "East Asian Miracle" — the emergence of rapid, sustained, internationally-oriented economic growth in East Asia. It provided an important part of the framework for an unprecedented and continuing era of trade expansion and, by historical standards, prosperity, encompassing larger and larger proportions of the world's population over time.

The Uruguay Round had considerable success in repairing the weaknesses in the old GATT — on the incorporation of agriculture within the rules; on the phasing out of the multi-fibres arrangement; on the reduction of developing country exemptions; on new issues; and on reducing the substantial residue of tariffs left over from earlier multilateral negotiations. It launched the WTO from a high base of achievement.

Nevertheless, an objective view of the GATT/WTO system on the eve of the Singapore Ministerial meeting would be as impressive for the problems that remain within it as for the recent achievements and immediate promise.

Four problems stand out above others.

First, the countries excluded from the WTO have become much more important in the international system, are rapidly becoming more important still, and there are no signs of their acceptance into the system. China and Taiwan are the most important of the exclusions, with China likely to be the world's fourth largest trading economy by the time the Uruguay Round commitments have been implemented, and possibly the largest a few decades into the twenty-first century.

Second, the developed countries' agenda for extension of the trading rules has run ahead of analysis, and therefore much further ahead of any foreseeable consensus on how to proceed, risking the bogging down of any new set of negotiations in profitless confrontation.

Third, and related to the second, changes in the content and style of leadership and public discussion of trade policy in the United States, and the enlargement in the United States appetite for extension of the international trade rules, have interacted with the domestic realization of diminishing relative economic power to corrode the United States' capacity for leadership of new change.

Fourth, there having been no progress in reforming the rules for regional free trade in the Uruguay Round, the liberal multilateral system remains vulnerable to the proliferation and extension of discriminatory regional blocs.

The challenge of the Singapore Ministerial Meeting is to find a way forward with multilateral trade liberalization, building on the success of the Uruguay Round in an environment in which the system's weaknesses are large and potentially damaging.

The Emergence of the Western Pacific Paradigm

Western Pacific economies have implemented major programmes of trade liberalization over the past decade. This has reinforced powerful tendencies towards strong economic growth and underwritten trade expansion.

One outcome is that the Western Pacific region has dominated the expansion of world inter-regional trade over the past decade. This gives it new weight and influence in the international system, which will expand further as rapid internationally-oriented economic growth continues.

The Western Pacific contributed two fifths of the expansion in the real value of total world imports from 1985 to 1994 (Table 6.1, Figure 6.1), when it had represented only one quarter of the total at the beginning of the period (Table 6.2). If we divide the world into four regional groupings — the European Union, NAFTA, Western Pacific and (amorphously) the Rest of the World, the

FIGURE 6.1
Real Imports, 1985–94

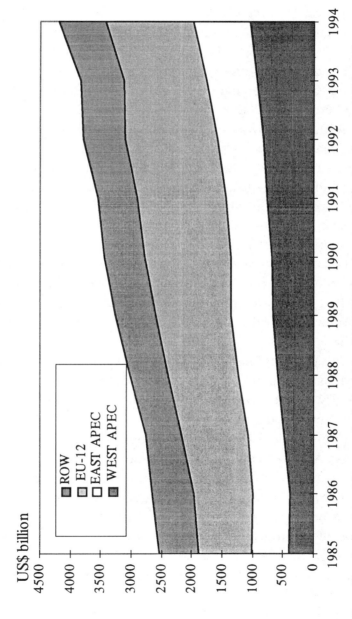

Note: Nominal value of imports is deflated by GATT/WTO unit value index for exports (1990=100).
Source: UN trade data, International Economic Databank, Australian National University.

Western Pacific absorbed two thirds of the expansion in the real value of Eastern Pacific APEC (North America plus Chile) inter-regional exports, and two fifths of the expansion for the European Union (Table 6.1). The Western Pacific absorbed three times as much as the European Union of the increment in North American exports. It absorbed over three times as much as North America of the increment in European Union exports.

Table 6.1 shows that the larger part of the large expansion of international world trade 1985–94 was internal to one or other of three regions — the Western Pacific, North America and the European Union. Intra-Western Pacific trade grew by more than intra-European and almost three times as much as intra-North American. Three fifths of the expansion of Western Pacific exports was to other Western Pacific economies.

On a global scale, Table 6.1 also highlights the special role of the European Union in the trade expansion of the "Rest of the World", notably that associated with structural transformation of formerly centrally planned economies in Eastern Europe and the CIS.

The Western Pacific has played an even more prominent role in expansion of global trade in the goods that had created greatest difficulty for the GATT — labour-intensive manufactures and agricultural products.

Export-oriented growth in the densely populated economies of East Asia was built in every case upon rapid expansion of labour-intensive exports — especially garments and textiles, but over time a wider range of simple products. East Asia has contributed a large part of the huge expansion of global exports over the period of rapid growth (Figure 6.2). The trading in this way of abundant and cheap labour for scarce capital and raw materials was important to the establishment of growth momentum at first in Japan and Hong Kong, and then successively in Taiwan, Korea, Singapore and Malaysia (although the latter two in smaller degree),

Thailand, China, Indonesia and most recently Vietnam and the Philippines.

Successful export-oriented growth made labour relatively less abundant. Wages and land rents rose, corroding comparative advantage in labour-intensive activities, and forcing structural change, towards production and export of more capital-intensive and technologically sophisticated products. Western Pacific economies generally maintained open import regimes for labour-intensive goods as their competitiveness declined: none joined the Multifibre Arrangement as an importer. One after another of the earlier participants in East Asian style growth began to import simple manufactures and shift their old and uncompetitive capacity

FIGURE 6.2
World Imports, East and South Asian Exports of
Labour-Intensive Manufactures, 1970–94
(US$ millions)

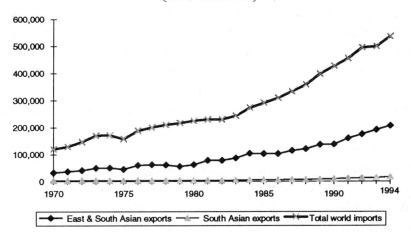

Notes: Nominal values of exports and imports are deflated by GATT/WTO unit value index for manufacturing exports (1990=100).
Source: UN trade data, International Economic Databank, Australian National University.

into lower-income economies — in the 1990s overwhelmingly into China. East Asia, once the smallest importer of labour-intensive goods amongst the four groups of countries identified above, swiftly overtook North America and the "Rest of the World" (Figure 6.3). The continued rapid expansion of exports from relative newcomers to the East Asian growth process was accommodated increasingly not from increased total imports to inter-regional markets in advanced countries (although these did grow considerably), but through taking over the market shares of and expanding exports to higher-income East Asian economies.

The decline in Japanese net exports accommodated much of the increase in labour-intensive exports from the newly industrialized economies (NIEs) in the 1970s and early 1980s (Figure 6.4). The decline in the NIEs' net exports accommodated much of the increment in Chinese exports over the past decade. Now, labour scarcity, rising wages and structural change in coastal China is widening export opportunities for inland China, Indonesia, Vietnam, the Philippines and South Asia. Thus acceptance of open trade and structural change in labour-intensive products within East Asia itself has eased the strains on the global trading system associated with successful internationally-oriented growth.

Nevertheless, North America in particular has continued to expand its net imports alongside continuing increases in net exports from East Asia (Figure 6.5).

The Western Pacific's role in world agricultural trade is the mirror image of that in labour-intensive goods. Notwithstanding the comparative agricultural strengths of Australia, New Zealand and Papua New Guinea in the Southwest Pacific, the region as a whole has a strong comparative disadvantage in commodities whose production requires agricultural land resources. The disadvantage has emerged in one after another East Asian economy in the process of sustaining rapid growth, as rising domestic incomes and demand have made it impossible to maintain self sufficiency

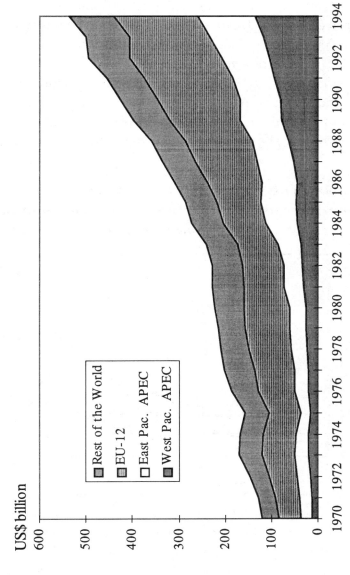

FIGURE 6.3
Labour-Intensive Imports, 1970–94

US$ billion

Rest of the World
EU-12
East Pac. APEC
West Pac. APEC

Note: Nominal value of imports is deflated by GATT/WTO unit value index for exports (1990=100).

Source: UN trade data, International Economic Databank, Australian National University.

while holding prices at or below international levels. At this crucial point in agricultural development in a densely populated economy, at which growing domestic demand pushes domestic prices above world prices, Japan, Taiwan, Korea and over the past two years China have opted for trade restriction rather than the holding of domestic prices at international levels.

Nevertheless, East Asia's comparative disadvantage in agricultural production at higher living standards has been so large that it has outweighed the effects of increasing agricultural trade restriction. The region has contributed the most rapid import

FIGURE 6.4

Ratio of Net Exports to World Imports of Labour-Intensive Manufactures, East and South Asia, 1970–94 (In percentages)

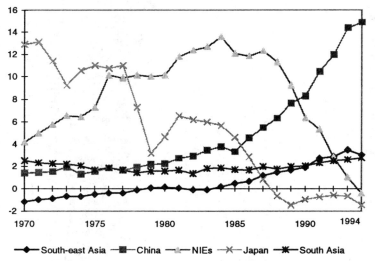

Notes: Southeast Asia includes ASEAN (excluding Singapore) and Vietnam; NIEs include Taiwan, Hong Kong, Korea and Singapore; and South Asia includes India, Pakistan, Bangladesh and Sri Lanka.

Source: UN trade data, International Economic Databank, Australian National University.

FIGURE 6.5

Net Export of Labour-Intensive Goods, 1970–94

(US$ billions)

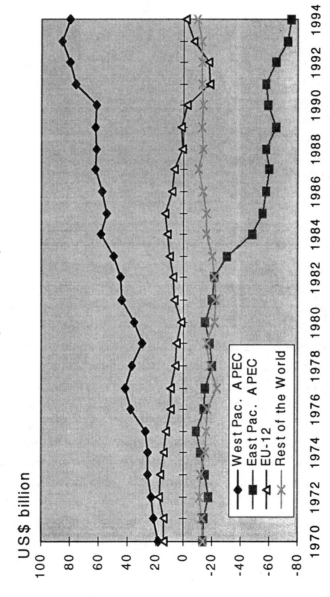

Note: Nominal value of imports is deflated by GATT/WTO unit value index for exports (1990=100).

Source: UN trade data, International Economic Databank, Australian National University.

expansion for agricultural imports (Figure 6.6), and has become the world's dominant net importing region (Figure 6.7).

The increased relative weight of the Western Pacific in world trade reflects sustained rapid economic growth and increasing openness and integration into the international economy. Rapid economic growth has a long way to go before it has run its course. The region's two most populous economies, China and Indonesia, after a decade of successful export-oriented industrialization, will each grow rapidly for several decades yet. Some populous economies in the region, notably Vietnam and the Philippines, have only recently put their feet on the lower echelons of the escalator of internationally-oriented industrialization.

Western Pacific Trade Liberalization

The process of reducing barriers to external trade and payments and deepening integration into the international economy has proceeded rapidly over the past decade throughout the Western Pacific. As with growth itself, it still has a long way to go, and therefore still holds large promise for expansion of global trade.

Far-reaching trade liberalization has occurred in all but two of the substantial Western Pacific economies over the past decade. The exceptions are Hong Kong and Singapore, which were the closest to free trade of all the world's economies throughout the period. The brilliant success of Hong Kong and Singapore encouraged the idea that free trade was in the interests of the open economy — Hong Kong having grown more than any other economy in the world since the early post-war period, and Singapore having grown more than any other since separation in 1965 ended the slight and brief flirtation with protection within Malaysia.

Western Pacific liberalization was overwhelmingly unilateral, undertaken because the liberalizing economies recognized that it was in their own interests. The largest liberalization was in the

FIGURE 6.6

Agriculture-Intensive Imports, 1970–94

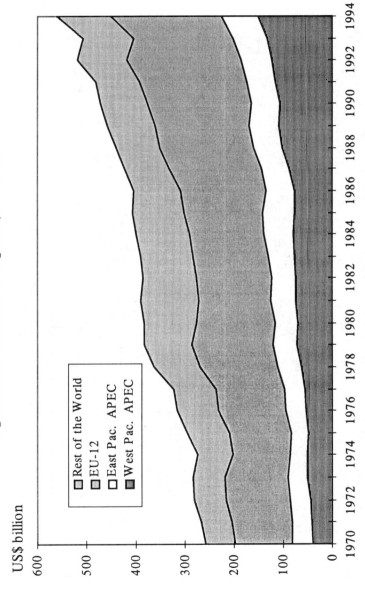

Note: Nominal value of imports is deflated by GATT/WTO unit value index for exports (1990=100).

Source: UN trade data, International Economic Databank, Australian National University.

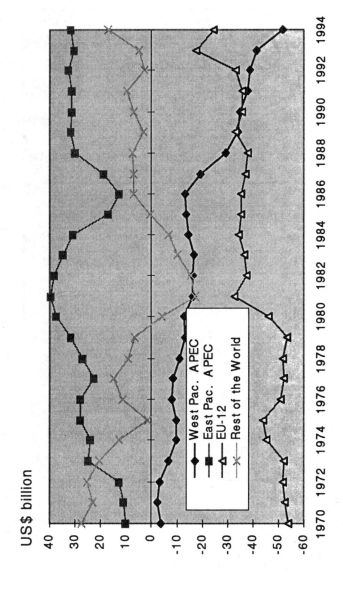

FIGURE 6.7

Net Export of Agriculture-Intensive Goods, 1970–94

Note: Nominal value of imports is deflated by GATT/WTO unit value index for exports (1990=100).

Source: UN trade data, International Economic Databank, Australian National University.

economies that had been the most closed at the outset: China and later Vietnam as they dismantled communist autarchy and central planning; and Indonesia as it responded to realization that export-oriented industrialization must drive growth as prospects for expanded oil revenues diminished from the mid-1980s.

Australia and New Zealand had the most protected manufacturing sectors amongst advanced economies in the OECD in the early 1980s. After a decade of reductions in protection, driven by domestic economic strategy but reinforced by recognition that liberalization at home increased credibility in calls for liberalization abroad, these two economies are now amongst the most open advanced economies.

Early in the 1980s, Australia and New Zealand executed the Closer Economic Relations (CER) agreement, providing for clean free trade across all goods and a wide range of services. In its immediate effect this was highly discriminatory, but much less so over time as external barriers were reduced rapidly in both economies. Tariff bindings offered in the Uruguay Round in both economies were generally at or higher than rates already announced, and so were not part of the process of reduction of protection.

In the ASEAN economies not mentioned so far, especially Malaysia, Thailand, Indonesia and the Philippines, reduction in protection has been accepted as an integral part of export-oriented growth strategies. There have been cross-currents and exceptions, but the general trend in protection has been steadily downward. The motive has been domestic economic strategy. Again in the ASEAN countries, bindings offered in the Uruguay Round were generally at or above levels already announced, with commitments affecting protection rates substantially only for some agricultural products. The formation of the ASEAN Free Trade Area (AFTA) in the early 1990s has in practice reinforced tendencies to external liberalization: Malaysia thoroughly and explicitly and others more or less and implicitly, have minimized discrimination against outsiders as the external tariff has been reduced within AFTA.

The story is a bit more complex in the other Northeast Asian economies — in Japan, Taiwan and Korea. Manufacturing sector trade liberalization over the past decade (two for Japan) has been far-reaching in each, with low protection by the early 1990s. This largely followed domestic economic strategy, although multilateral trade negotiations had direct effects in Japan and Korea and some influence in Taiwan. Unilateral threats and pressures from the United States as well as the processes of the Uruguay Round were important in securing significant but limited liberalization of agricultural trade.

The Pacific Economic Co-operation Council's assessment of changes in tariff and non-tariff protection in the Western Pacific and Eastern Pacific APEC countries are summarized in a recent report (PECC 1995). Average tariffs have come down much faster in the Western Pacific, but remain higher. The incidence of non-tariff barriers (NTBs) is higher in the Eastern Pacific, and has come down rapidly but less than in the Western Pacific. This illustrates one practical effect of the divergence between Eastern and Western Pacific paradigms over the past decade.

Free and Open Trade in the Asia-Pacific

Asia-Pacific Economic Co-operation has brought together and required reconciliation of the different trade policy tendencies and paradigms currently dominant respectively in the Western and Eastern Pacific.

The divergence is far from absolute. There are examples of Western Pacific behaviour in the East. Some of the most entrenched areas of protection in the United States and Canada — for example, agricultural export subsidies — are now proving themselves to be to some extent amenable to imperatives of domestic economic strategy, and in particular to the need to reduce the budget deficit. Chile, and to a lesser extent Mexico, have engaged in far-reaching unilateral liberalization over the past decade. In the West, China has tended to respond to "tit for tat" trade policy pressures in an Eastern Pacific manner, at times holding back liberalization for a while as bargaining coin, and diverting imports to competitors of the United States.

At the APEC Summit at Bogor in 1994, Leaders committed themselves to an end point of complete free trade by 2010 for developed and 2020 for developing economies. At the APEC Summit in Osaka in 1995, Leaders committed themselves to a process of moving towards the end point, involving informal understandings and application of the most-favoured-nation principle, rather than discrimination under Article 24 of the GATT. The commitments were within the Western Pacific paradigm, many would argue because it was superior in its effects. In any case, the alternative, a formal and binding commitment to free trade including a schedule and timetable for reductions in protection under Article 24 of the GATT, was simply not practicable on either side of the Pacific. It was not practicable in the Eastern Pacific because, at least, the United States polity had no appetite for major new free trade commitments of a binding nature, least of all with Japan and China. And it was not practicable in the Western Pacific because major economies (notably Japan, Indonesia and China) were wary of major exercises in trade discrimination.

The asymmetry in approach across the Pacific carries two large practical implications for the realization of APEC's free trade commitments. First, success will depend on continued substantial trade liberalization in Western Pacific economies, so the United States polity can come to see its own future liberalization as reciprocating steps that have already been taken elsewhere. Second, success is more likely and more secure if APEC commitments are joined by others, especially in the European Union, so that North American liberalization within APEC is seen within a wider framework of (albeit diffuse and informal) reciprocity.

The Singapore Ministerial Meeting

It will not be easy simply to proceed to another multilateral round from Singapore, within the old GATT paradigm. The most important issues involve non-members of WTO (China); it is not the time for the now traditional leadership from the United States in multilateral negotiations; and we are a long way from consensus on the appropriate approach to a range of new issues that some influential members would want to be part of a new round of multilateral negotiations.

Obviously at Singapore there will be review of progress on implementing Uruguay Round commitments and on the in-built agenda left over from the Uruguay Round. But that alone would be less than a disappointing start.

The way to do better is to bring the Western Pacific paradigm to account in Singapore.

The Singapore meeting would start to bring it to account by recognizing the central role that the Western Pacific now plays in global trade liberalization and expansion.

It is a short step from this realization, to recognition of the urgency of China and Taiwan membership of the WTO — rather more urgency and importance than in progress on any particular issue in a likely agenda for negotiations.

Recognition of the Western Pacific region's contemporary role in the global system would lay a basis for general commitment to a goal of free trade and for trade liberalization towards that goal, without stalling on-going processes of liberalization as each country defines objectives and begins to accumulate coin for a long negotiation. The latter process might be inevitable and necessary if trade liberalization itself had no life, and if there were no alternative to the old-style reciprocity. But unilateral liberalization in the Western Pacific, and now concerted unilateralism within APEC, have created an alternative.

Others, bound by requirements of reciprocity can now make the Western Pacific liberalization, and commitment within APEC ultimately to free trade, as the basis for commitments of their own to liberalization towards free trade. This is, in effect, what implementation of APEC's Bogor Declaration requires from North America. APEC's Bogor Declaration can provide a basis for a matching commitment from the European Union — conditional, if it likes, on continued progress within APEC. There is sufficient momentum towards East Asian-style unilateral liberalization in developing countries elsewhere, partly in emulation of the East Asian example, for these steps in APEC and Europe to establish momentum towards global free trade by 2010 or 2020.

These steps are feasible in November without being preceded by lengthy formal negotiations. Are they of any use without mechanisms for legal enforcement? We will learn the answer from the progress of APEC in the period ahead. But where a major region in world trade — now the largest centre of trade expansion — is leading the way, without prior negotiation and commitment by others, the possibilities expand.

Successive commitments to an objective of free trade by 2010 and 2020 would be mutually reinforcing. A European commitment would facilitate United States political support for the APEC free trade goal. This, in turn, would reduce the risk of trans-Pacific tension knocking Western Pacific unilateral liberalization off course.

All of this might be seen as "shallow integration" — the completion of work on the Uruguay Round. Pressure would remain for expansion of the agenda. But the new issues would be handled on their merits, without becoming reasons for declining opportunities for progress on the old, which remain immensely important to global welfare, and on which much remains to be done.

7
THE ASIA-PACIFIC
Role Model and Engine of Growth

Over the past half century, populous communities in East Asia have experienced faster economic growth sustained over long periods than had previously been known in any large part of humanity. This has transformed the world economy, with East Asia joining Western Europe and North America as one of three main centres of global production and trade. East Asia has become the world's largest source of surplus savings for international investment, and the world's most voracious importer of foodstuffs and raw materials.

The half century over which this transformation has occurred is not such a short period. It is roughly the time that lapsed between the conclusion of the Civil War and American entry into World War I — which was the time over which rapid industrialization transformed the United States into the world's greatest economic power. It is not much less than the time from Adam Smith's creation of *The Wealth of Nations* to the repeal of the Corn Laws, over

---

This chapter was first presented at the International Monetary Conference in Sydney in June 1996.

which the industrial revolution transformed Britain from an important European nation, to the main centre of global economic and military power.

The time over which sustained rapid economic growth has been occurring in East Asia is not so short in modern historical terms, and yet the process remains in its earlier stages. If the end point is the enjoyment throughout East Asia of the average output levels and incomes at that future time in the old industrial economies, then the process has run less than a quarter of its course in terms of output growth, and probably no more than half of its time. While total output in East Asia now exceeds that in Western Europe or North America, on the most generous of estimates only about 15 per cent of the people of East Asia, nearly half of them in Japan, yet enjoy productivity and income levels comparable with averages in the old centres of industrial civilization in the West. Most of the others lag a very long way behind the global frontiers.

The awesome and exciting reality is that we have yet seen only the early part of the economic modernization of East Asia. On my reading of the evidence, it will continue several decades and more into the next century, by which time the vast populations of the Chinese inland, of Java, of Vietnam and the Philippines will enjoy living standards now dreamed of only by small elites in each of their countries. At that time, in the middle of the twenty-first century, the global economy will have at its centre a large, dense, prosperous East Asia, contributing production of more than twice the volume of goods and services of North America and Western Europe together.

By that time — itself no further in the future than the opening stanzas of post-war economic growth is in the past — East Asia's relative position in the world economy will have passed its peak. Failing some great catastrophe, some huge failing of organized humanity, the recent stirrings of internationally-oriented economic growth in South Asia, by then home to as many people as East

Asia itself, will have gathered large momentum, to that exciting stage of economic growth where swift movement is made towards the world's frontiers.

I share these thoughts on the past and the future to place the phenomenon of sustained, rapid growth in East Asia into perspective. The growth phenomenon has put East Asia on a course many parameters of which were followed earlier in the old industrial economies. It is faster than anything known elsewhere, but that is at least partly because an economy can move more quickly when it is bridging a large gap between its own productivity levels and the world frontiers. East Asian output will end up being quantitatively more impressive than North American or European, but mainly because more of humanity inhabits this East Asian Hemisphere. The process will not end at the boundaries of East Asia, and this region's great economic achievements may later be followed and challenged from South Asia and elsewhere.

East Asia in the Asia-Pacific

Within the geographic limits that are set for Asia-Pacific Economic Co-operation (APEC), almost half the 18-economy membership is not East Asian. There are three Southwest Pacific and four American countries. It is the East Asian rather than the Asia-Pacific economy that has experienced sustained rapid growth over the past half century. But there is nevertheless an Asia-Pacific community, linked by intensive trade and investment ties, and now by commitment within APEC to a distinctive approach to international economic policy.

Australia, especially, and now Papua New Guinea and New Zealand, have been profoundly influenced by East Asian economic growth. It transformed their economic opportunities and influenced their international economic strategies. The share of Australian exports going to East Asia is higher than for any economy in

East Asia itself. Australian thought about East Asian development and Asia-Pacific economic co-operation, focused by the high stakes that Australia has in these issues, have carried influence and weight in regional affairs.

The United States' role in the process of East Asian growth has been crucial — to its beginning, and to its sustenance. The United States provided the strategic framework in which internationally-oriented growth took root and prospered in island and peninsula Northeast Asia, and to a considerable extent Southeast Asia. The United States was the leader and the guarantor of the post-war international trading system based on the General Agreement on Tariffs and Trade, within which there was rapid export expansion and structural change in foreign trade in one after another East Asian economy. And the United States provided an explicit and acknowledged model for the development of economic institutions in East Asian economies, particularly in the influential cases of Japan, Taiwan and Korea, at least until success nurtured confidence in indigenous inventions after several decades. More recently, North America economies and economic strategy have themselves been strongly influenced by East Asian trade and investment opportunities, especially over the past decade since the value of trans Pacific trade first exceeded trans Atlantic.

The United States ceased to provide the major part of the growth in East Asian export markets more than a decade ago. That role is now played by intra-regional trade within East Asia itself (Table 7.1 and Chapter 6, Table 6.1). But the United States continues to play a crucial part in regional affairs: the absolute size of its market remains considerable; its financial markets and advice remain highly influential in most important new developments in the Asia-Pacific economy; it continues to generate a high proportion of the technological innovation in industries producing high value goods and services; it is the source of a high proportion of the new ideas about business management and organization that are

TABLE 7.1

Increase in East Asia's Exports to Various Destinations, 1985–95

(US$ billions)

	World	North America	EU-15	ASEAN	East Asia Chinese Economies	East Asia Total	East Asia % of World
Japan	235.7	60.1	46.7	65.1	54.4	143.8	61.0
Korea	85.7	13.9	10.6	14.9	20.7	47.3	55.2
China	121.0	26.1	16.0	5.8	36.2	69.0	57.1
Hong Kong	137.1	30.9	21.1	9.6	50.9	71.6	52.2
Taiwan	81.1	14.7	10.1	10.7	23.5	44.3	54.6
Indonesia	26.7	3.7	5.8	5.1	5.0	16.5	61.7
Malaysia	54.6	13.8	8.1	15.7	8.0	29.9	54.8
Philippines	12.5	5.2	2.0	1.6	1.2	5.5	44.2
Singapore	58.7	12.5	9.6	14.0	12.7	32.4	55.3
Thailand	47.9	9.7	6.7	9.2	4.7	22.9	47.7
Vietnam	4.8	0.2	1.3	0.6	0.7	2.9	59.8
Papua New Guinea	1.7	0.0	0.0	0.2	0.1	0.9	51.1
Australia	26.9	1.6	2.4	6.5	4.8	20.8	77.3
New Zealand	8.1	0.8	0.8	0.8	0.9	3.7	46.0
Chinese economies	339.2	71.8	47.1	26.1	110.6	184.9	54.5
ASEAN	205.2	45.0	33.5	46.2	32.3	110.1	53.7
All Western Pacific	902.5	193.3	141.1	159.8	223.7	511.6	56.7

Source: Asia-Pacific Economics Group, *Asia-Pacific Profiles 1996* (Canberra: Australian National University 1996).

discussed seriously through East Asia; and its best universities and research institutes continue to train and to socialise a substantial proportion of East Asian business and political elites.

For all of these reasons, there is an Asia-Pacific as well as an East Asian community. The search for a framework to conserve and enhance the process of deepening economic co-operation within the Asia-Pacific, and the tensions deriving from divergent perspectives across the Pacific, have generated ideas about international economic co-operation that are becoming highly influential in the world trading system. More of that later.

An East Asian or Asia-Pacific Role Model?

The East Asian and, more so, the Asia-Pacific experience of economic growth is highly diverse, across economies and across time. Australia, the United States, New Zealand and Canada were amongst the first economies in the world to become rich from internationally-oriented growth and, having been rich early, have observed others catching up with them over the past half century. The United States more than other early-rich economies embraced competitive markets relatively little encumbered by government intervention, and a public sector of modest scale. This distinction of the United States diminished during the New Deal; and was qualified by high protection until the United States led the industrial economies in reducing barriers to international trade in the post-war period.

The other old rich Asia-Pacific economies are now more American than European in these respects, although one would have been less certain of this judgement a decade or more ago. In these respects, they have also become more East Asian. It is a brave generalization, but it can be said that Asia-Pacific and not only East Asian or United States economic growth is distinguished from the European by greater reliance on private sector initiative, competitive markets and flexible prices and industrial structures.

In at least small part, this reflects the persuasive presence of the United States in Western Pacific development at crucial historical points.

But when there is reference to an Asia-Pacific pattern of economic growth, and questions about an Asia-Pacific role model, it is inspired by the post-war experience of East Asia rather than the wider Asia-Pacific — the so-called "East Asian economic miracle".

It seemed miraculous when Japan more than doubled output through the 1950s and announced that it would repeat the performance in the 1960s. Hong Kong and Taiwan began their long periods of rapid growth at about the same time, but were not noticed until much later. Korea followed from the early 1960, and Singapore a few years on. Malaysia and Thailand have sustained rapid growth from the early 1970s, and most impressively and consistently over the past decade. The beginnings of China's sustained rapid growth is usually dated precisely, to the third plenum of the Eleventh Central Committee of the Communist Party in 1978, which for the first time gave decisive support to reform and opening to the outside world. Indonesia's sustained rapid growth came in two stages, the first from the late 1960s fuelled by petroleum exports, followed by more typically East Asian growth based on rapid expansion of manufactured exports from the mid-1980s. Unambiguous commitment to internationally-oriented growth in Vietnam was triggered by the collapse of the Soviet Union and Comecon in 1989. The Philippines has found it difficult to hold to policies necessary for sustained growth, but has shown strong signs of getting closer over the past few years.

One need do no more than list the East Asian economies that have sustained rapid growth over the past decade, to draw attention to the heterogeneity of their economic and political systems and of their economic experience. What is now clear is that there is nothing miraculous about sustained rapid growth in East Asia. It occurs in a wide range of institutional settings once a number of conditions have been met. There is continuing debate about the necessary conditions, although less controversy as the growth experience and analysis move on.

This is my list of the necessary and the helpful conditions of sustained rapid economic growth in the East Asian style.

The most basic condition is that there must be an effective State, capable of delivering stable economic policies and a range of public services necessary for development against the pressures of international and domestic interest groups. Amongst the services that the effective State must be able to deliver, is enforcement of the security of property and contract that underpins market exchange. This condition might seem so obvious and simply met that its specification does little to illuminate the prospects for growth. This is not the case. The absence of this condition in most developing countries explains many instances of development failure.

Closely related is a requirement that the community, the polity, must have come to assign high, usually pre-eminent priority to the objective of economic growth. Rapid economic growth sustained over long periods is disruptive and destructive of established elites, interests, institutions and ways. The disruption if not the growth itself generates resistance, which eventually stalls the process unless it is confronted by a determined government with broadly based support for its growth-oriented policies.

Political cohesion and stability around the growth objective is achieved more securely when there is wide distribution of the benefits of and opportunities to participate in growth. Publicly provided or assisted basic education and health services, sometimes housing, and in Northeast Asia land reform have each played a role in strengthening the political base for sustained rapid growth. It seems to have helped that almost all the East Asian economies that have sustained rapid growth over long periods have been densely populated by world standards. Their comparative advantage in international trade at an early stage of their economic development has therefore been in labour-intensive production processes, which have expanded rapidly as the economy has been opened to the outside world. This has been associated with increases in employment and labour incomes, thus effecting wide distribution of the benefits of growth.

A closely related requirement is the maintenance of a reasonable degree of economic stability — reasonably low inflation, convertibility of the currency, moderation in foreign and domestic official debt. These conditions, of course, themselves require recognition of the importance of economic stability, and the presence or the capacity to build institutions and operatives that are necessary to deliver economic stability over long periods.

The sustained growth that has been experienced in one after another East Asian economy over the past half century is in an important sense a rapid "catching up" with the world's most technologically and economically advanced societies. This is only possible while there is a considerable gap — explaining why some of the newly industrialized economies (NIEs) were able to move even faster than Japan for at least part of their period of rapid growth, and why the coastal areas of China have moved most rapidly of all. Growth has slowed when the international frontiers have been approached — Japan in the mid-1970s, and Hong Kong, Taiwan and now Singapore in the 1990s.

Rapid catching up with the world's economic frontiers requires a number of other conditions to be met. It requires a high degree of openness to foreign trade and payments, and as a necessary support, the avoidance of wide disparity between policy-induced incentives for import-replacement and export production. Openness to foreign technology, management and ideas is similarly important. It requires high rates of savings and investment, including investment in broadly based education, a condition that becomes more demanding at higher levels of development and economic evolution into more technologically sophisticated and capital-intensive activities.

Finally, sustained rapid growth over long periods, and the bridging of a wide development gap from the world's economic frontiers over a relatively short period of time, require acceptance of continuing large and rapid changes in industrial structure. This, in turn, requires acceptance of a large role for markets in resource allocation, and the integration of domestic into international markets for goods and services.

This is my list of the common conditions for sustained rapid growth in the East Asian style. Other conditions are often put forward; but none of these is present across the range of East Asian economies.

It must be said that it helps to be located in East Asia itself. The powerful expansion of trade and investment opportunities in East Asia over recent decades have been most readily and cheaply available to economies within and adjacent to the region. More importantly, the influence of the East Asian experience on aspirations for growth and on growth policies is most powerful within the region itself and in adjacent regions.

This takes us to the first question that I address in this paper: is the Asia-Pacific (read "East Asia") a role model?

My answer is yes, on some issues. The demonstration that sustained rapid growth can be achieved by many economies once certain conditions are met, has proven to be irresistible to one after another East Asian society. The Japanese experience was powerful in the development of Taiwan and Korean development strategy. Japanese and especially Hong Kong and Taiwan experience exerted powerful influence on Chinese economic reform from the 1970s. The leading Southeast Asian growth economies absorbed much from Northeast Asia. And the die of aspiration if not achievement was cast for Vietnam and the Philippines, and now in North Korea, by the economic success of their neighbours.

Now that we understand better the common and the necessary conditions for sustained economic growth in the East Asian style, these have been pursued more assiduously by East Asian economies seeking growth.

As the story of East Asian growth has been clarified by experience and analysis, it has become more influential outside its own region. It has played a role in the increased international orientation of Latin American economic policies over the past decade. It, and especially the challenging example of China, has been critical to reform in India over the past five years (Garnaut 1996). It will become influential more widely as success in India and parts of Latin America demonstrate that East Asian style economic success is not confined by nature, history or culture to the region of its origin.

There is nothing uniquely or even especially East Asian about the conditions for East Asian growth that I have specified. In the 1920s, most of them might have been thought of as especially American, and the America-based international institutions and the American graduate schools to which they are closely connected promote many of them today as good economic policy. So an important part of East Asia's role as model, properly applied, is to underline the rewards from what might be considered more generally as good and prudent economic policy — cautious fiscal policy, open trade and payments, use of markets, acceptance of structural change as growth proceeds, and high levels of savings and investment including in education.

At least in the Asia-Pacific region, the East Asian example has helped to re-establish support for some of these old virtues in the old industrial economies — not least in Australia, the economy that has been most intimately connected through trade to East Asian growth.

The Asia-Pacific as an Engine of Growth

The sustained economic growth of East Asia over recent decades, and the even more rapid expansion of trade, has made East Asia the main centre of world trade expansion.

The region's relative scarcity of natural resources has caused it greatly to increase demands on global and especially Asia-Pacific foodstuffs and raw materials for several decades. It was the industrialization and growing imports of Japan that conferred commercial value on Australian iron ore, non-ferrous mineral and energy resources through the 1960s and 1970s, spurred resource exports from Southeast Asia, and gave the initial impetus to export growth from China under the open policies.

The most advanced economies of the region came to provide a more general and powerful source of trade growth for others from the mid-1980s, when real exchange rate appreciation at first in Japan, and then in Hong Kong, Singapore, Taiwan and Korea triggered the movement offshore of a large part of the labour-intensive manufacturing industries that had been located in these economies.

The adjustments of the mid- and late-1980s saw Japanese direct investment in manufacturing rise sharply in the NIEs, China and the ASEAN economies. The process went further under the influence of the strong yen through the later stages of the Japanese recession in the 1990s. Total Japanese imports rose from US$ 118 billion in 1985 to US$ 293 billion in 1995, disproportionately focused on manufactured goods from East Asia. Illustrating the dimensions of the continuing structural change, Japanese imports in United States dollars rose by 47% between 1992 and 1995, over the recession years in which Japanese GDP increased by a total of less than 2%.

The Japanese adjustment, encompassing yen appreciation, trade liberalization and a more effective role for market forces in reducing transactions costs in Japanese international trade, supported rapid upgrading of exports and industrial structure out of labour-intensive manufactured goods in the NIEs. This, in turn, expanded the opportunity for rapid expansion of labour-intensive manufactured goods from China and the ASEAN economies. The NIEs became net importers of labour-intensive manufactured goods in 1994, providing a large part of the market opportunities required by export growth in China and ASEAN without corresponding pressure on import expansion and structural adjustment in the old industrial economies (Chapter 6, Figure 6.4).

It was the explosive rate of structural change in the Northeast Asian NIEs (Hong Kong, Taiwan and Korea) that was the most powerful external trigger for the China boom of the first half of the 1990s. Chinese real output expanded by 58% in four years from 1991 to 1995, exports by 107% in United States dollars, and imports also by 107%.

Structural adjustment in the NIEs fuelled the China boom through the expansion of trade opportunities observed in Figure 7.1, and also through direct investment. China became the recipient of by far the largest flow of direct investment ever recorded to a developing economy and after the United States, the second largest to any country in recent years (Table 7.2), overwhelmingly from Hong Kong, Taiwan and Korea.

The China boom of the 1990s sustained rapid export expansion and economic growth in the East Asian developing economies (that is, East Asia outside Japan) through the OECD recession. Weighted average output growth in East Asian developing economies was close to its highest levels ever in 1992 (9.5%), 1993 (10.1%) and 1994 (10.1%). This is an historic development in the story of East Asian economic growth, underlining the extent to which East Asian growth is now able to sustain itself, independently of

FIGURE 7.1
East Asian Economies Way Out in Front

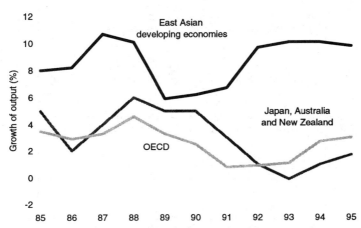

Source: Asia-Pacific Economics Group, *Asia-Pacific Profiles 1996* (Canberra: Australian National University, 1996).

growth in the old industrial economies. For the first time since it all began in the early post-war period, rapid growth in the East Asian developing economies kept going through an OECD recession (Figure 7.1).

Economic growth and structural change stimulated trade expansion well beyond East Asia itself, especially but not only in the Asia-Pacific region. Global trade expansion since the mid-1980s has been characterized by disproportionately strong growth in intra-regional trade, and rising intra-regional shares in total trade. This is obviously true in East Asia, and perhaps less obviously but also powerfully within the European Union, within North America and within Australia-New Zealand Closer Economic Relations.

The one exception involves trade with East Asia. The share of East Asia in exports and total trade has expanded in Western

TABLE 7.2

Foreign Direct Investment Inflows to East Asian Developing Economies

	1985	1986	1987	1988	1989	1990	1991	1992	1993	1994	1995
China	1.7	1.9	2.3	3.2	3.4	3.5	4.4	11.2	27.5	33.8	36.0
Indonesia	0.3	0.3	0.4	0.6	0.7	1.1	1.5	1.8	2.0	4.6	7.7
Japan	0.6	0.2	1.2	-0.5	-1.1	1.8	1.4	2.7	0.1	0.9	1.1
Korea	0.2	0.4	0.6	1.0	1.1	0.8	1.2	0.7	0.6	0.8	0.9
Malaysia	0.7	0.5	0.4	0.7	1.7	2.3	4.0	5.2	5.0	4.3	5.2
Philippines	–	0.1	0.3	0.9	0.6	0.5	0.5	0.2	0.8	1.7	1.8
Singapore	1.0	1.7	2.8	3.7	2.9	5.6	4.9	2.4	5.0	5.6	5.6
Thailand	0.2	0.3	0.4	1.1	1.8	2.4	2.0	2.1	1.7	1.1	1.4
Taiwan	0.3	0.5	0.7	1.0	2.4	2.3	1.8	1.5	1.2	1.6	2.9
Hong Kong	0.3	0.3	0.3	0.3	0.3	0.3	0.2	0.3	0.3	0.3	0.4
Vietnam	–	–	–	–	0.1	0.2	0.3	0.5	1.0	1.5	2.0
India	–	–	0.2	0.3	0.4	0.1	0.2	0.4	0.9	1.0	1.5
Total	5.3	6.2	9.4	12.0	13.9	20.8	22.2	29.9	45.2	56.2	65.0

Source: Asia-Pacific Economics Group, *Asia-Pacific Profiles 1996* (Canberra: Australian National University 1996).

Europe, in North America, in Oceania, and in much of the rest of the world. Trade with East Asia is the dynamic element in inter-continental world trade (Figure 7.2).

⌈This is the central sense in which East Asia has become an engine of global growth. Structural change and export expansion in East Asia can now keep going. And they are the source of continuing dynamism in inter-continental trade at a time when global trade expansion is heavily intra-regional. They are expanding the opportunities for continued structural change and growth in the old successful economies.⌉

⌈There are other ways in which East Asia has been an engine of global growth over the past decade. I shall touch upon a few of the more important of them. The prodigious savings of East Asia have generated substantial surpluses beyond East Asia's own high requirements for investment, especially in Japan, Taiwan

FIGURE 7.2

East Asia's Increasing Importance in World Trade

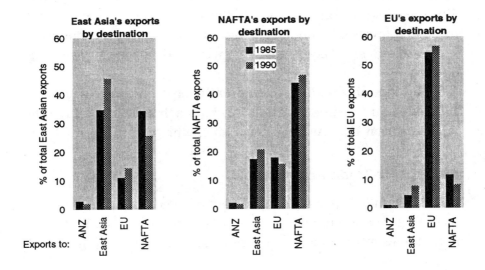

Source: Asia-Pacific Economics Group 1996.

and Singapore, and from time to time in Korea, China and Hong Kong. This has provided resources for investment elsewhere at a time when the rest of the world has been unable to support high levels of investment from its own savings. Without the high savings and current account surpluses in East Asia, there would have been stronger upward pressure on global interest rates, constraining investment and growth in highly indebted countries (including in Oceania and North America) and in developing economies generally. This was especially important during the deficit-led United States boom of the early- and mid-1980s. It is not helpful to global economic growth that total East Asian surpluses are now in decline (Asia-Pacific Economics Group 1996), and fortunate that the United States is reducing its demands on international capital markets through fiscal consolidation at this time.

East Asia has brought some distinctive comparative strengths into the global economy, including a facility for early and efficient mass production of goods incorporating new technology. This has extended global frontiers of production and consumption. The East Asian example and challenge has elevated ambitions for higher levels of economic achievement amongst communities in the old industrial economies that were in the process of settling for less.

But it is above all through greatly expanding opportunities for trade and for specialization in what each country and region does best that East Asia has been an engine of global growth.

Asia-Pacific Trade and the WTO

I shall conclude with a few remarks about some distinctive features of foreign economic policy in the Asia-Pacific region, and their potential for providing a helpful model for the future of the world trading system.

All but three of the Western Pacific economies that are

participants in Asia-Pacific Economic Co-operation have implemented far-reaching trade liberalization over the past decade: Australia and New Zealand; the ASEAN economies (including Vietnam which is not yet a member of APEC); Japan; Korea; Taiwan; and, most dramatically of all in its effects, China. The exceptions are Hong Kong and Singapore, which already had virtual free trade, and Papua New Guinea. Amongst the liberalizing economies there has been some/ambiguity and backsliding from time to time, but the general tendency is clear and strong.

That is not to say that any of the Western Pacific economies other than Hong Kong and Singapore practice free trade. Agricultural protection is high by world standards in Japan, Taiwan and Korea, and manufacturing protection still considerable in China and Southeast Asia.

But the process of liberalization has gone a long way and has much momentum right through the Western Pacific.

Regional trading arrangements in the Western Pacific have been implemented in the context of multilateral liberalization. Closer economic relations between Australia and New Zealand abolished trade barriers between them in the 1980s, and both rapidly dismantled barriers to trade with third countries soon after they established their free trade area. ASEAN heads of government in 1991 agreed to establish an ASEAN Free Trade Area covering most trade by 2003, and their progress so far towards this goal has been matched in each member country by reduction in trade barriers against third countries.

A distinctive feature of trade liberalization in the Western Pacific over the past decade is that it has been overwhelmingly unilateral, undertaken because each country judged that it was in the best interests of its own development. All East Asian APEC members other than China and Taiwan are members of GATT as well and all participated in the Uruguay Round — but at least for Southeast Asia and Oceania, the Uruguay Round commitments fell short of announced unilateral liberalization. The Uruguay Round bit deeper in Northeast Asian agriculture, and bilateral pressure from the United States forced the pace on some issues in Northeast Asia with symbolic but quantitatively modest importance.

The trade liberalization of each Western Pacific economy has benefited its own development, but also expanded the gains from liberalization in others. Liberalization and trade expansion across the region have therefore been mutually reinforcing, both economically and politically.

What has emerged as the Western Pacific approach to trade liberalization contrasts sharply with the ethos of trade negotiations among the old industrial economies, embodied in GATT. There, trade liberalization is seen as a concession, to be yielded only in response to corresponding "concessions" by others. The result is formal and enforceable agreements, long and slow negotiations, sometimes holding back as negotiating coin steps that might otherwise be taken in the normal progress of domestic economic policy.

These contrasting trade policy paradigms had to be reconciled before progress could be made in the implementation of Asia-Pacific Economic Co-operation's ambitions for free trade by 2010 (for developed countries) and 2020 (for developing). It was accepted at the Osaka APEC Leaders' meeting in 1995 that the Western Pacific approach, around the new concept of *"open regionalism"* would be the way forward. There was, in reality, no alternative, because a formally negotiated free trade area on the model of NAFTA or the European Union is simply not practicable in the Asia-Pacific.

We will now see whether the approach to trade liberalization that has been so productive in the Western Pacific over the past decade, can be effective in a wider area.

This is a test for Asia-Pacific Economic Co-operation as much as for the Western Pacific trade paradigm, as the APEC commitment to regional free trade cannot be taken forward in any other way. The onus is on the Western Pacific economies, as the United States polity is in no mood to lead in breaking new ground in free international trade.

The tests will come together late in 1996, when Southeast Asia becomes for a while the centre of the world discussion. The Philippines hosts the APEC Leaders' Summit in November, in the immediate aftermath of the United States Presidential election. In December, Singapore hosts the inaugural ministerial meeting of the World Trade Organization. The APEC meeting will receive and consider the "action programmes" of individual economies, towards the agreed goal of free trade by 2010 or 2020. The WTO meeting will review implementation of the Uruguay Round, and define the way forward for the global trading system.

Philippine policy analyst and adviser, Jesus Estanislao, provided some insights on ASEAN thinking about these pivotal meetings to the Asia-Pacific Profiles conference in Hong Kong in May 1996. Estanislao advised the Conference that ASEAN leaders were considering the tabling of a joint "action programme" at the Manila Summit, embodying the multilateralization of the commitments to free trade within ASEAN by 2003. The hope was that this major initiative in *open regionalism* would spur liberalizing responses in other APEC members, which could then be taken to the Singapore WTO meeting as a basis for global free trade.

These are bold thoughts, building on the realities of East Asian economic growth and trade expansion of the past decade. If they survive to Singapore they would offer the world trading system a goal and an ethos that could do much to transfer to the world as a whole the approach to trade liberalization that has been productive in the Western Pacific.

The Asia-Pacific would then have become a role model for the global trading system on a scale commensurate with its considerable economic achievements.

8
A PACIFIC FREE TRADE AREA?

I Introduction

Vigorous expansion of trade, investment and other economic ties within the East Asian and Pacific economy have been crucially important to the region's extraordinary growth in recent decades. This expansion has taken place without the framework of formal regional institutional arrangements that fostered integration across the Atlantic among the original OECD countries (Crawford and Okita 1976, p.34). The growth of Pacific economic integration represents an impressive example of "market integration" around institutional and legal barriers to trade capital movements and other forms of economic interchange.[1] Integration has occurred despite persistent political resistance to the domestic structural implications of internationally oriented growth. In the course of

This chapter was jointly authored with Peter Drysdale. It was first presented at a conference at the Institute for International Economics, Washington D.C., in September 1988. It was first published as Drysdale and Garnaut (1989) and is reproduced here with the permission of the Institute of International Economics.

growth, some barriers have been lowered, others have been introduced anew, or raised, and many remain.

This chapter takes as the central objective of international economic diplomacy in the Pacific region, the preservation and enhancement of the conditions for continued economic growth in the style of recent decades. The international system that has supported vigorous trade expansion is under threat from several directions: tension between the United States and Japan (and to a lesser extent between the United States and Taiwan and Korea) over large trade and payments imbalances; the prospect of increased economic introversion in Europe as 1992 approaches; the accommodation of new patterns of comparative advantage in the Asian newly industrialized economies (NIEs) as they compress adjustments to a decade of rapid economic growth into a few years; and the new challenge of managing the emergence of China, with its partly reformed centrally planned system, as a major player in Pacific economic relations. It is important for peace and political stability, too, that the environment of relatively open economic relations that made a realistic alternative to autarky available to China at a crucial point in its political history is preserved to provide similarly reliable alternatives for the states of Indochina, the Soviet Union and the Democratic People's Republic of Korea (DPRK), at a time of opportunity for progress on reducing long-standing sources of conflict.

The central objective is thus a conservative one: to preserve the current system of relatively open economic relations in the Pacific, however imperfect that may be. We would then add, as second and third objectives, the reduction of barriers to intra-Pacific trade, and the reduction of trade and other barriers to enhanced economic relations with major economies outside the region, particularly the European Communities.

This paper examines whether these objectives would be promoted by the formation of a Pacific Free Trade Area.

One question that must be addressed is whether the central, conservative objective can be achieved without progress on the second and third objectives. Frustration at the lack of progress in reducing Northeast Asian and European barriers to trade, especially on agricultural products, has been an important element in the erosion of political support in the United States and elsewhere for the multilateral system. We can expect this frustration to intensify if the Uruguay Round delivers disappointing results.

We have been asked to assess the merits of and prospects for a free trade area encompassing the market economies of the Western Pacific, together with those of the United States and Canada. Trade and other economic relations among these countries have been characterized by high intensity and rapid growth. They are thus a convenient group of economies to consider in this context. The role of the People's Republic of China must also be discussed as a trading economy similar in scale of total trade to Taiwan and the Republic of Korea, experiencing similarly rapid growth, specialized in labour-intensive manufactured exports in the early style of other Northeast Asian economies, and oriented to the Pacific region in its foreign economic relations.

Thus when, for brevity, we refer to "the Pacific region", we include the United States, Canada, the Western Pacific market economies, and the People's Republic of China. Later we make separate reference to the circumstances of Mexico, lacking close economic ties across the Pacific but trading intensively with the United States, and to the centrally planned economies of the Western Pacific, which as yet have only slender economic links with their Pacific neighbours.

II Pacific Trade and Growth

East Asian economies in recent decades have experienced stronger growth than the world had previously known on a sustained basis.

From the mid-1950s, Japan grew at a rate that more than doubled output each decade, until, by the time of the first oil shock, its production per capita was close to the frontiers of the world industrial economy. The four Asian NIEs started their high growth later, in the early 1960s, and from lower bases than Japan, but on average have grown even more rapidly. Three of them, Taiwan, Singapore and Hong Kong, have already surpassed the average per capita output in lower-income OECD countries. Korea, starting from a lower base, still seems likely to attain the living standards of OECD laggards before the end of the century.

Over the past decade, China has jointed the ranks of the high-growth East Asian economies. It has been exceeding the goal that it set itself, to double real output each decade.

In the principal ASEAN economies other than Singapore, that is, Indonesia, the Philippines, Thailand and Malaysia, growth has been less consistent and more modest, but has comfortably exceeded average performance for world developed and developing economies alike since the late 1960s.

Japan's growth since it broadly "caught up" with productivity levels elsewhere in the OECD in the mid-1970s has been less spectacular, but has remained above the average for advanced economies.

One result has been a historic shift in the centre of gravity of world production. In the early post-war period, when the liberal trading system around GATT was being established, North America accounted for one half of world GNP, and East Asia, devastated by war and civil strife, for only a few per cent. By the early 1960s, the North American share of world production was still extremely large, around 40 per cent, but East Asia's share had increased to 9 per cent. By the early 1980s, North America's share of world GNP had fallen to 27 per cent but East Asia's had more than doubled, to 19 per cent. These trends have continued, and it seems that in the 1990s East Asia will contribute as much as North America

TABLE 8.1

Resource Endowments, Sectoral Shares of Total Trade and "Revealed" Comparative Advantage in Developed and Developing Pacific Countries, 1986[a]

	Australasia[b]	North America[c]	Japan	China	Asian NIEs	Other ASEAN	Industrial Market Economies	Developing Economies[d]
Population density (persons per km²)	2.4	13.8	326.8	110.2	507.0	95.4	24.0	53.0
GNP per capita (US$)	11,157	17,158	12,840	300	3,308	647	12,960	610
Real GNP per capita growth rate, 1965–86 (per cent per annum)	1.7	1.7	4.3	5.1	6.8	4.0	2.3	2.9
Sectoral shares of total trade (per cent)								
Agriculture								
Exports	47	18	1	22	7	34	14	22
Imports	8	9	26	10	14	13	14	16
Fuels, minerals and metals								
Exports	35	10	1	16	6	35	8	35
Imports	7	12	41	4	16	15	17	11
Light manufactures								
Exports	3	5	10	45	47	14	11	25
Imports	15	14	8	14	18	11	11	14

TABLE 8.1 (cont'd)

	Australasia[b]	North America[c]	Japan	China	Asian NIEs	Other ASEAN	Industrial Market Economies	Developing Economies[d]
Heavy Manufactures								
Exports	15	67	88	17	40	17	67	20
Imports	70	65	25	72	52	61	56	57
"Revealed" comparative advantage								
Agriculture	3.3	1.2	0.1	1.6	0.5	2.3	0.9	1.4
Fuels, minerals and metals	2.2	0.7	0.1	1.0	0.4	2.3	0.6	2.2
Light manufactures	0.3	0.4	0.8	3.4	3.1	1.1	0.9	1.6
Heavy manufactures	0.3	1.1	1.6	0.3	0.8	0.3	1.2	0.4

Notes: [a] Exports and imports refer to export and import shares, respectively. "Revealed" comparative advantage is defined as the ratio of the share of a commodity group in total exports for a country or group of countries to that commodity share of world exports.
  [b] Australia and New Zealand
  [c] United States and Canada
  [d] Excludes high-income oil exporters

Sources: Drysdale (1988): updated from the International Monetary Fund and World Bank, *World Development Report* (New York: Oxford University Press, 1988).

TABLE 8.2
Pacific and World Trade Shares, 1965 and 1987
(Per cent)

Reporter		Australia and New Zealand 1965	1987	Japan 1965	1987	Other Northeast Asia 1965	1987	ASEAN 1965	1987	China 1965	1987	North America 1965	1987	Pacific Total 1965	1987	Western Europe 1965	1987	Middle East 1965	1987	Mexico 1965	1987	Latin America 1965	1987	Rest of the World 1965	1987
Australia & NZ	X	6.2	8.2	14.4	24.8	1.9	7.2	1.3	6.7	4.5	3.9	13.3	14.4	44.8	68.2	44.4	19.8	1.7	4.5	0.5	0.2	1.2	1.4	7.9	6.1
	M	5.6	7.6	9.3	20.4	1.1	4.7	2.0	5.4	0.6	1.7	25.8	23.3	45.1	63.8	45.3	29.4	4.6	2.9	0.1	0.2	0.5	1.2	4.4	2.7
Japan	X	5.0	2.9	–	–	6.1	10.2	8.8	7.2	3.2	3.8	35.7	41.4	58.9	65.7	14.2	20.9	3.8	4.0	0.5	0.6	5.9	3.7	17.2	5.7
	M	8.0	6.4	–	–	1.0	6.8	6.9	13.8	2.9	5.2	35.3	26.5	54.5	58.2	9.4	15.9	13.9	14.1	1.9	1.1	9.2	4.3	13.0	6.7
Other Northeast Asia[a]	X	3.8	1.9	9.5	11.8	1.4	3.8	6.4	5.4	1.1	12.2	34.6	37.2	57.0	72.2	28.6	18.2	2.5	3.1	0.2	0.2	2.0	2.0	9.8	4.6
	M	2.2	2.6	23.0	27.8	0.9	3.1	3.8	7.7	21.3	18.3	19.6	17.2	70.7	76.8	20.6	14.8	1.6	3.5	0.3	0.3	1.6	1.9	5.5	2.8
ASEAN	X	3.7	2.6	24.0	21.9	3.4	7.9	2.9	16.8	2.2	2.4	29.3	23.4	65.6	74.7	25.1	15.6	0.8	2.8	0.0	0.0	0.8	0.9	7.6	5.3
	M	2.1	3.2	27.9	24.9	2.2	5.7	5.0	16.1	4.5	4.2	23.8	16.4	65.5	70.1	24.8	18.1	2.9	7.6	0.3	0.1	0.6	1.0	6.2	2.6
China	X	2.1	0.9	15.9	16.2	28.8	34.9	7.1	5.9	–	–	1.1	8.7	55.0	66.7	23.5	11.4	3.2	6.5	0.0	0.0	0.3	1.2	17.9	14.3
	M	13.3	3.6	19.0	23.7	1.0	19.8	3.1	4.8	–	–	7.5	14.6	44.0	66.7	27.3	20.7	2.0	0.9	0.2	0.2	7.5	2.9	19.3	8.9
North America[b]	X	3.1	2.1	6.8	10.0	1.4	4.0	1.5	3.2	0.3	1.4	29.6	38.3	42.7	58.9	31.4	22.7	3.0	3.6	3.3	4.5	13.3	11.0	9.7	3.9
	M	1.7	1.0	9.1	19.2	1.5	6.3	2.0	3.8	0.1	1.5	36.2	27.9	50.5	59.7	25.2	22.8	1.8	2.7	2.3	4.4	16.8	10.6	5.6	4.2
Pacific Total[c]	*X*	*3.7*	*2.5*	*7.3*	*9.5*	*2.9*	*7.7*	*2.9*	*6.1*	*1.1*	*3.4*	*28.6*	*35.2*	*46.8*	*64.5*	*29.4*	*20.4*	*2.9*	*3.7*	*2.4*	*2.1*	*10.1*	*6.1*	*10.8*	*5.2*
	M	*3.6*	*2.8*	*9.3*	*17.6*	*1.4*	*6.6*	*3.0*	*6.9*	*1.6*	*3.9*	*32.9*	*24.8*	*51.9*	*62.5*	*24.6*	*20.7*	*4.0*	*5.0*	*1.8*	*2.7*	*12.5*	*7.2*	*7.0*	*4.5*
Western Europe	X	2.2	0.8	0.8	1.7	0.5	1.1	0.7	1.1	0.5	0.7	9.5	9.8	14.3	15.2	65.0	71.4	3.0	3.8	0.5	0.2	4.1	2.1	13.7	7.5
	M	2.2	0.6	1.2	4.6	0.5	1.5	0.6	1.2	0.4	0.6	13.5	7.6	18.4	16.2	57.8	70.7	4.8	2.8	0.3	0.3	5.5	2.4	13.6	7.8

TABLE 8.2 (cont'd)

Reporter		Australia and New Zealand 1965	1987	Japan 1965	1987	Other Northeast Asia 1965	1987	ASEAN 1965	1987	China 1965	1987	North America 1965	1987	Pacific Total 1965	1987	Western Europe 1965	1987	Middle East 1965	1987	Mexico 1965	1987	Latin America 1965	1987	Rest of the World 1965	1987
Middle East	X	3.0	1.1	13.6	23.7	0.6	3.5	0.9	6.6	0.4	0.4	7.9	15.2	26.3	50.5	53.7	37.4	9.1	4.5	0.0	0.0	1.7	4.2	9.1	3.5
	M	1.5	2.0	5.4	12.4	0.5	3.6	0.2	2.7	0.9	2.1	18.2	14.2	26.8	36.9	47.3	55.6	13.7	4.7	0.0	0.0	0.8	0.7	11.4	2.2
Mexico	X	0.4	0.2	8.2	5.9	0.2	0.9	0.4	0.4	0.3	0.3	64.2	76.7	73.6	84.3	9.4	13.3	0.1	0.0	–	–	8.5	2.1	8.4	0.2
	M	1.3	0.3	2.5	7.3	0.1	0.9	0.0	0.2	0.0	0.1	68.4	77.5	72.3	86.1	24.5	12.8	0.0	0.1	–	–	2.6	0.5	0.7	0.5
Latin America[d]	X	0.2	0.4	4.0	6.2	0.2	1.3	0.2	0.7	0.8	1.2	38.2	53.3	43.7	63.2	34.7	27.1	0.4	0.5	0.2	0.1	17.0	7.2	4.2	1.9
	M	0.6	0.6	3.8	8.0	0.2	2.1	0.2	0.8	0.0	0.8	42.0	45.3	46.8	57.5	30.0	28.0	1.5	4.4	0.7	0.7	19.4	8.2	2.3	2.0
Rest of World	X	1.0	0.5	4.3	6.7	0.6	1.6	0.5	1.3	1.4	2.6	8.0	13.7	15.8	26.3	57.2	61.1	2.9	1.4	0.1	0.1	1.3	1.0	22.8	10.1
	M	1.4	1.4	6.0	9.0	0.6	2.7	0.7	2.8	1.1	3.8	15.9	9.3	25.7	29.0	49.6	58.5	2.3	2.2	0.4	0.0	2.4	1.2	20.1	9.2
World	X	2.4	1.4	3.9	5.8	1.2	3.6	1.3	3.1	0.8	1.8	17.2	21.1	27.0	36.9	50.6	49.3	3.0	3.5	1.0	0.9	6.5	3.8	13.0	6.5
	M	2.4	1.5	4.4	10.2	0.7	3.6	1.3	3.5	0.8	2.1	21.1	15.8	30.7	36.8	45.4	48.9	4.3	3.7	0.7	1.2	7.8	4.3	11.8	6.3

Notes: X = exports.
M = imports.
[a] Korea, Taiwan and Hong Kong.
[b] United States and Canada.
[c] Australia, New Zealand, Japan, Other Northeast Asia, ASEAN, China, North America and the Pacific Islands.
[d] Includes Mexico, the Caribbean and other Latin American countries.
Source: IMF, *Direction of Trade Statistics;* and International Economic Databank, Australian National University.

to world GNP, with the two regions accounting for over one half of world output.[2]

These shifts in the locus of world economic power have implications for the leadership and management of the international trading system, and these are addressed later in the chapter.

East Asia's growth in recent decades has been associated with a certain style of relations with the international economy. The share of trade in output has expanded rapidly. The early years of rapid growth have been associated with powerful specialization in the export of labour-intensive manufactures, but patterns of export specialization have then progressed rapidly to more capital-intensive production with growth in living standards. Trade growth has been geographically focused in the Pacific region.

These trends, and some reasons for them, are illustrated in Tables 8.1 and 8.2.

Table 8.1 demonstrates the vast potential for intra-Pacific trade based on differences in relative endowments of natural resources, labour and capital. The theory of changing comparative advantage in the process of economic growth postulates that a poor country will initially have comparative advantage in production of natural resource-based products; that growth of the capital stock will cause comparative advantage to shift towards labour-intensive manufacture and services if the country's per capita natural resource endowment is poor, but not otherwise; and that continued growth, shown by higher per capita income, will cause comparative advantage to shift successively to more capital-intensive manufactures and services.[3]

This pattern has been demonstrated by the growth experience of the Pacific region. Wide variations in per capita natural resources endowments, represented crudely by population density in Table 8.1, suggest high complementarity between Australasia and North America on the one hand, and East Asia particularly Japan and the Asian NIEs, on the other. The large variations in per capita income provide opportunities for trading capital-intensive for labour-intensive manufactures. And the ascension of Japan and several of the NIEs to the ranks of relatively high-income economies is opening rich new opportunities for intra-industry specialization in trade in technologically sophisticated goods and services, especially amongst the adjacent economies of Northeast Asia.

A distinctive feature of high growth in East Asia has been the rising shares of foreign trade in production, as the economies of the region put to good use the potential gains from trade deriving from widely different relative resource endowments. East Asian and Pacific trade is growing more rapidly than world trade. The dollar value of Europe-North America two-way trade increased slightly more than sixfold between the beginning of the 1970s and 1987; Japan-North America trade increased almost tenfold; trade between Japan and the newly industrializing countries of Northeast Asia increased eighteenfold; and trade between North America and the Northeast Asian countries jumped more than forty-eightfold in the same period. (Data drawn from International Monetary Fund 1988). Already, the East Asian and Pacific region accounts for 37 per cent of total world trade.

The huge economic transformation that has been taking place in East Asia has brought with it a major shift towards the Pacific and away from the Atlantic as the focus of world trade. Table 8.2 sets out changes in the geographic structure of Pacific and world trade flows between 1965 and 1987. Over this period, the Pacific share in world trade grew from around 30 per cent to almost 37 per cent. Intra-regional trade grew from less than 50 per cent to around 63 per cent in the Pacific countries. The latter proportion approached that of Europe's intra-regional trade: in 1987, intra-regional trade amounted to 71 per cent of Western Europe's total trade. Pacific countries' trade with each other is almost twice as large as their share in world trade. For Australasia, Korea, Taiwan, Hong Kong, ASEAN and China, the share of other Pacific countries in export and import trade is commonly higher, around 70 per cent.

III Barriers to Pacific Trade

The trade expansion that has supported East Asian growth and structural change is a historic achievement of the international system. Nevertheless, old and new barriers have prevented realization of substantial potential gains from trade amongst Pacific countries.

Rapid economic growth has generated rapid change in comparative advantage in the East Asian economies and in their trading partners. The general record of structural adjustment in response to changing comparative advantage has been a good one — as attested by the expansion and change in commodity composition of trade. But there are important instances of governments in East Asia and elsewhere in the Pacific intervening to block the structural implications of growth.

The major instances of high protection causing potential gains from intra-Pacific trade to dissipate all occur in large industries that were rapidly losing comparative advantage as a result of economic change in Northeast Asia. Principal examples from industries producing goods include foodstuffs in Japan, Korea and Taiwan, and labour-intensive commodities (textiles, clothing and footwear, and consumer electronics) and standard technology manufacturing industries (metals, motor vehicles) in North America and Australasia.

The outstanding example of barriers to intra-Pacific trade is provided by Northeast Asian agricultural protection (Table 8.3). In the period covered by the table, Australia had negative protection for all agriculture. The United States had no protection on average for agriculture but high protection for sugar in the first half of the 1980s. The introduction of the export enhancement programme and other agricultural assistance in recent years would have modified this picture, but leaving average United States assistance to agriculture at moderate levels in international terms. Japan, Korea and Taiwan, by contrast, provide extraordinarily high levels of assistance for all agriculture, and for the commodities that are of greatest importance in Pacific trade. The major liberalization of Japanese beef imports announced in 1988 will significantly moderate protection for this commodity.

Amongst Pacific countries not represented in Table 8.3, New Zealand, following major liberalization initiatives since 1984, provides virtually no assistance to agriculture. Canada generally provides low protection to agriculture, although dairy products, and to a lesser extent sugar, are exceptions (Hathaway 1987, p.91). China and the ASEAN countries have highly distorted agriculture, but at current international prices probably low net assistance. In

TABLE 8.3
Selected Pacific Countries' Agricultural Protection, 1980
(Per cent)

	Australia	United States	Japan	Korea	Taiwan
Rice	−12	3	192	156	135
Wheat	−6	−18	261	33	81
Barley	−14	−5	307	90	73
Sugar	−1	45	141	–	−3
Beef	−1	5	100	67	76
Agriculture	−2	0	85	117	52

Notes: These figures are rates of agricultural protection, defined as the percentage by which the producer price exceeds the border price. The estimates shown are the weighted averages for twelve commodities, using production valued at border prices as weights.
Source: Anderson and Hayami (1986, Tables 2.5 and 2.6).

the case of China — important amongst other reasons for being the world's largest producer and consumer of grains, a range of other foodstuffs, and agricultural raw materials — there may be little or no net assistance to the foodstuffs that are most important in current consumption, but high protection for meat and other high quality foodstuffs, which are increasingly important in consumption as incomes rise.

By comparison, the European countries' assistance for agriculture is very high, but well below the levels in Japan, Korea and Taiwan (Hathaway 1987, p.91).

The general pattern of protection in manufacturing is more complex and less easily summarized. Average tariff levels are now low in the United States, Canada and Japan, although by no means negligible in all commodities.[4] Low nominal rates of tariffs nevertheless provide substantial effective protection for some metals and metal products where little value is added in the manufacturing process.

Average rates of nominal tariff protection on all industrial products are much higher in Korea (23.5 per cent) and Taiwan (13.8 per cent).[5] Highly protected categories in Korea include machinery and transport equipment (21.4 per cent), chemicals (21.4 per cent) and miscellaneous manufactures (28.2 per cent) in Taiwan, highly protected categories include textiles (16 per cent), machinery and transport equipment (14.5 per cent) and chemicals (14.2 per cent).

Australia and New Zealand for some years have had the highest average tariff levels on manufactured goods of all OECD countries (Anderson and Garnaut 1987). Recent policy initiatives have reduced rates substantially, but averages remain high by OECD standards, although lower than for Korea and Taiwan. After the implementation of recently announced liberalization measures (Keating 1988), tariffs in Australia will remain very high only for textiles, clothing, footwear and passenger motor vehicles (up to 35 per cent). New Zealand tariffs remain especially high for a similar range of goods.

The proliferation of non-tariff protection devices during and since the mid-1970s recession has caused tariffs to be a most unreliable guide to manufacturing protection levels. Over this period the United States has introduced major non-tariff protective devices in textiles, apparel, footwear, steel, automobiles and motorcycles, and consumer electronic goods (television and radios) (Hufbauer and Rosen 1986). Recent policy initiatives have left Australia and New Zealand relatively clear of non-tariff barriers for manufactured goods. In Australia, quantitative restrictions in the form of tariff quotas (the main non-tariff barriers) now apply only to textiles, clothing and footwear. These restrictions are being phased out in an announced series of steps that will end in 1995.

Contrary to international perceptions, Japan has the cleanest import system for manufactured goods amongst OECD countries; official non-tariff barriers have almost no effect on trade.[6] The relatively low proportion of manufactured goods in Japanese imports, and low import penetration ratios in manufactured commodities of which other developed countries are major importers, have led protectionist interests in North America, Europe and Australasia, and sometimes officials and independent commentators in those same countries, to postulate a major role for non-official barriers, perhaps with official sanction. It is true that the Japanese distribution systems contain powerful conservative bias, delaying the emergence of large-scale imports well beyond the time when imports appear to have become competitive. Such biases are not unique to Japan (Itoh 1988). Moreover, the evidence since the appreciation of the yen in 1985 suggests that, despite long lags, the normal competitive pressures operate for Japan. Japan's imports of manufactured goods from Asian developing countries have been increasing at around 50 per cent per annum since 1985. The share of manufactures in Japanese total imports has also been increasing rapidly over this period, although not so strongly from the United States (see Table 8.4).[7]

Non-tariff barriers are high for manufactured goods in Korea and Taiwan, although liberalizing steps are being taken in both these economies.

Manufacturing production in China and other ASEAN countries is highly distorted by protection in the forms of high tariffs, quantitative restrictions and local content schemes. In China and the Philippines this is exacerbated by exchange controls, and in China by a large proportion of production still being allocated at arbitrary prices through state corporations.

Recent attempts to measure protection in the other ASEAN countries have generated figures like 109 per cent effective protection for import-competing manufacturing in Indonesia (Pangestu and Boediono 1986, p.25), 36 per cent effective protection for all manufacturing in the Philippines (Tan 1986, p.65) and 50 per cent (Corden method) or 71 per cent (Balassa) effective protection on importable manufacturing in Thailand (Akrasanee and Ajanant 1986, p.94).[8] Malaysian average effective protection is probably close to the lowest in other ASEAN for manufacturing as a whole, but the most recent estimates suggest very high levels for such large categories as non-durable consumer goods (85 per cent) consumer durables (173 per cent) and machinery (39 per cent) (Hock 1986, p.120).

Each of the other ASEAN countries has attempted major liberalization over the past decade. There has been some modest progress, particularly in Indonesia and Thailand, and some retrogression. The general picture of variable and extremely high protection remains.

China and ASEAN countries (other than Singapore) would benefit greatly by participation in international trade negotiations

TABLE 8.4
Japan: Share of Manufactured Goods in Total Imports, 1979–88
(Per cent)

		Share in all imports	Share in imports from the United States	Share in imports from Australia
1979		26.0	42.3	8.8
1980		22.8	44.1	9.2
1981		24.3	45.3	10.0
1982		24.9	47.4	8.6
1983		26.6	52.4	10.5
1984		29.8	52.0	11.7
1985		31.0	55.2	12.9
1986		41.8	60.7	18.0
1987		44.1	56.1	22.5
1988	January	45.0	56.4	29.0
	February	48.8	61.9	26.1
	March	47.7	56.0	23.9
	April	49.9	55.1	33.0
	May	48.6	54.1	26.6
	June	48.2	56.3	23.0
	July	46.8	52.9	25.9
	August	49.2	51.6	26.0

Note: Manufactured goods comprise the categories of "chemicals", Machinery and Equipment and "Others". Petroleum products are not included.
Source: Japan Tariff Association, *The Summary Report on Trade of Japan* (various issues).

that provided incentives on the export side of liberalization and rationalization of their import regimes. Indeed, the extension of East Asian high growth on a sustained basis to these important countries would seem to require such initiatives, which would also help to sustain growth elsewhere in the region.

TABLE 8.5
Pacific Commodity Exports and Imports, 1986
(In US$ millions, percentage of country/region's total exports/imports)

		Textiles, Clothing and Footwear		Domestic Electrical Equipment		Road Motor Vehicles		Iron and Steel		Non-Ferrous Metals		Unmilled Wheat		Unmilled Feedgrains[a]		Rice		Sugar[b]		Beef		Total Commodities
United States	X	3.605	1.8	510	0.3	18.514	9.1	1.081	0.5	1.841	0.9	3.006	1.5	3.265	1.6	621	0.3	–	–	606	0.3	204.654
	M	31.386	8.2	2.573	0.7	69.421	18.2	9.556	2.5	7.976	2.1	27	0.0	102	0.0	38	0.0	821	0.2	1.258	0.3	381.362
Canada	X	733	0.9	99	0.1	23.916	28.3	1.749	2.1	3.232	3.8	2.041	2.4	503	0.6	–	–	35	0.0	143	0.2	84.381
	M	3.795	4.8	614	0.8	21.696	27.3	1.386	1.7	812	1.0	0	0.0	79	0.1	42	0.1	195	0.2	187	0.2	79.631
Australia & NZ	X	351	1.3	50	0.2	184	0.7	439	1.6	1.615	6.0	1.915	7.2	427	1.6	58	0.2	454	1.7	1.446	5.4	26.749
	M	2.147	7.0	278	0.9	2.562	8.4	666	2.2	213	0.7	4	0.0	7	0.0	10	0.0	24	0.1	4	0.0	30.471
Japan	X	6.242	3.0	1.799	0.9	52.993	25.4	12.706	6.1	1.567	0.8	–	–	0	0.0	0	0.0	1	0.0	2	0.0	209.081
	M	5.520	4.6	104	0.1	1.398	1.2	1.762	1.5	3.655	3.1	886	0.7	2.358	2.0	4	0.0	338	0.3	553	0.5	119.424
Korea	X	10.740	31.0	583	1.7	1.514	4.4	1.971	5.7	143	0.4	–	–	0	0.0	0	0.0	54	0.2	0	0.0	34.702
	M	947	3.0	119	0.4	378	1.2	1.344	4.3	702	2.2	425	1.4	397	1.3	0	0.0	183	0.6	0	0.0	31.518
China	X	10.725	34.4	129	0.4	15	0.1	141	0.5	212	0.7	2	0.0	393	1.3	104	0.3	37	0.1	34	0.1	31.158
	M	2.572	7.9	145	0.4	1.402	4.3	4.411	13.5	570	1.7	607	1.9	88	0.3	43	0.1	40	0.1	91	0.0	32.720
Taiwan	X	10.234	25.9	601	1.5	616	1.6	566	1.4	132	0.3	–	–	0	0.0	20	0.1	30	0.1	–	–	39.486
	M	565	2.4	58	0.2	587	2.4	1.112	4.6	781	3.3	125	0.5	466	1.9	1	0.0	32	0.1	81	0.3	24.023
Hong Kong	X	8.228	41.7	624	3.2	2	0.0	16	0.1	37	0.2	–	–	–	–	–	–	1	0.0	–	–	19.734
	M	8.201	23.2	280	0.8	482	1.4	880	2.5	528	1.5	21	0.1	24	0.1	112	0.3	37	0.1	67	0.2	35.366

TABLE 8.5 (cont'd)

		Textiles, Clothing and Footwear		Domestic Electrical Equipment		Road Motor Vehicles		Iron and Steel		Non-Ferrous Metals		Unmilled Wheat		Unmilled Feedgrains[a]		Rice		Sugar[b]		Beef		Total Commodities
ASEAN	X	4.388	6.6	242	0.4	191	0.3	479	0.7	1.264	1.9	1	0.0	384	0.6	802	1.2	484	0.7	3	0.0	66.531
	M	2.644	4.2	220	0.4	1.606	2.6	2.611	4.2	858	1.4	545	0.9	150	0.2	119	0.2	183	0.3	67	0.1	62.399
World	X	142.815	7.2	11.751	0.6	194.610	9.8	68.696	3.5	38.916	2.0	11.328	0.6	10.147	0.5	2.743	0.1	4.840	0.2	8.182	0.4	1.984.670
	M	147.744	7.2	12.022	0.6	192.318	9.3	71.261	3.5	40.817	2.0	12.112	0.6	10.947	0.5	2.758	0.1	1.916	0.2	8.338	0.4	1.062.575
Pacific[c]	X	55.254	7.7	4.636	0.7	97.947	13.7	19.285	2.7	10.048	1.4	6.964	1.0	4.973	0.7	1.606	0.2	1.221	0.2	2.236	0.3	715.949
(US$ million)	M	57.856	7.3	4.403	0.6	99.706	12.5	23.764	3.0	16.102	2.0	2.658	0.3	3.674	0.5	365	0.1	1.860	0.2	2.243	0.3	798.199
Pacific Share	X	38.7		39.4		50.3		28.1		25.8		61.5		49.0		58.5		25.2		27.3		36.1
in World (%)	M	39.2		36.6		51.8		33.3		39.4		21.9		33.6		13.2		37.8		26.9		38.7
Pacific Share	X	52.4		56.9		67.1		38.5		33.7		78.7		67.4		69.4		28.4		51.4		46.7
in World less	M	52.1		53.0		68.5		45.4		51.2		27.7		44.9		15.2		41.6		49.2		49.3
Intra-EEC Trade (%)																						

Notes: [a] Unmilled barley, maize, rye, oats and other cereals (excluding wheat and rice).
[b] Raw beet and cane sugar, refined sugar, etc., and molasses.
[c] Pacific comprises the countries specified above and the Pacific island states.
– denotes a nil value or share.
0 denotes a value less than $500 thousand.
0.0 denotes a share less than 0.05 per cent.

Source: The International Economic Databank, Australian National University.

At a time when macroeconomic frustrations in the United States have been generating aggressive reactions against all of the successful economies in East Asia, it should not be neglected that two economies in the region, Singapore and Hong Kong, have by far the cleanest import systems in the world, with barely a hint of restriction against trade in goods, and relatively few barriers to trade in services.

For the higher income Pacific countries, protective barriers are highest in foodstuffs, textiles, clothing and footwear, and motor vehicles. They are significantly distorting in the production of domestic electrical equipment, iron and steel and (because of tariff escalation) non-ferrous metals.

Table 8.5 sets out in some detail participation in world trade in commodities in which some Pacific countries have high protection. A striking feature of the table is the tendency for Pacific countries' exports to be heavily concentrated in commodities against which other Pacific countries impose high barriers to trade.

Textiles, clothing and footwear accounted for a third of the total exports of Korea, mainland China and Hong Kong in 1986, a quarter of the exports of Taiwan, and a high proportion of ASEAN manufactured exports. Significantly, excluding intra-EEC trade from the total, Pacific countries account for more than one half of total world exports in these commodities. Despite high protection (matched by similarly high barriers elsewhere), Pacific countries account for a similar proportion of world imports.

A similar pattern emerges for trade in other commodities in which Pacific trade barriers are high. Excluding intra-EEC trade, Pacific countries account for two thirds of world motor vehicle exports. Amongst agricultural commodities, Pacific countries dominate world markets for wheat, feedgrains and rice, and supply half of the world's exports of beef. The proportion is lower for sugar of which tropical developing countries outside the Pacific are the important suppliers.

This pattern has not emerged by accident. All Pacific countries have moved to protect those industries in which they have most profoundly lost comparative advantage as a result of East Asian growth.

From these data we can draw the strong conclusion that, should Pacific countries reduce assistance to their most highly protected industries on a non-discriminatory basis, the associated expansion of exports is likely to be concentrated in other Pacific countries simply on grounds of competitiveness.

There is certainly considerable scope for further expansion of trade by Pacific countries through measures that provide more confident market access and that reduce the trade barriers that limit the realization of the potentially strong complementarity within the region. Given the relatively low resistances to regional trade reflected in regional trade concentration, the reduction of trade barriers on a most-favoured-nation basis, in a way that does not offend Pacific countries' global trading interests, is likely to mean that most new suppliers of imports will come from within the region rather than from non-Pacific countries.

The growth of East Asian and Pacific markets has made the major contribution to world trade growth over the past twenty years, and especially over the past decade. Table 8.6 reveals that net of intra-European trade, around 50 per cent of world trade growth in this period has been in the Pacific market.

Table 8.6 shows that Pacific markets have absorbed two thirds of the strong growth in East Asia's exports over the past two decades. East Asian import growth itself has absorbed one third of the total. The United States' role as a market was especially important in the decade from the mid-1970s recession, but has slowed since the macroeconomic adjustments of 1985. Europe's role as a market, though much smaller, was nevertheless too significant for East Asian countries to ignore as a focus of trade policy interest. It is noteworthy too, that Japan absorbed a

TABLE 8.6
Contributions to the Growth in World Trade, Excluding
Intra-EEC Trade, 1965–86
(Per cent)

Country		Share in World Trade			Contribution to World Trade Growth		
		1965	1975	1986	1965–75	1975–86	1965–86
Australia	X	2.1	1.7	1.4	1.6	1.1	1.3
	M	2.3	1.4	1.5	1.2	1.6	1.4
Japan	X	6.0	8.3	13.6	9.0	17.7	14.4
	M	5.6	8.4	7.4	9.2	6.6	7.6
China	X	1.2	0.9	2.0	0.9	2.9	2.1
	M	0.9	0.9	2.0	0.8	2.9	2.1
Other Northeast	X	1.1	2.2	6.1	2.6	9.1	6.6
Asia^a	M	1.8	2.9	5.6	3.2	7.6	6.0
ASEAN	X	3.1	3.3	4.3	3.3	5.2	4.5
	M	3.2	3.4	3.9	3.5	4.2	3.9
East Asia Total	X	*11.3*	*14.8*	*26.1*	*15.7*	*34.8*	*27.6*
	M	*11.5*	*15.6*	*18.9*	*16.7*	*21.3*	*19.6*
North America^b	X	24.9	20.7	18.8	19.6	17.4	18.2
	M	19.9	19.0	28.5	18.7	35.6	29.4
New Zealand and	X	0.8	0.5	0.5	0.4	0.5	0.4
other Pacific	M	1.0	0.7	0.5	0.6	0.4	0.5
Pacific Total^c	X	*39.1*	*37.6*	*46.7*	*37.2*	*53.6*	*47.4*
	M	*34.6*	*36.7*	*49.3*	*37.2*	*58.8*	*50.8*
EEC	X	23.5	21.9	22.0	21.4	22.2	21.9
	M	27.7	23.2	20.5	22.0	18.5	19.8
Middle East	X	5.2	11.4	4.9	13.1	–0.2	4.8
	M	3.4	6.0	4.7	6.8	3.8	4.9
Rest of World	X	32.2	29.1	26.4	28.3	24.3	25.8
	M	34.3	34.1	25.4	34.0	39.0	24.5

Notes: X = exports
  M = imports
  ^{a} Korea, Taiwan and Hong Kong
  ^{b} United States and Canada
  ^{c} Australia, New Zealand, Japan, Other Northeast Asia, ASEAN, China,
North America and the Pacific Islands
Source: International Economic Databank, Australian National University.

TABLE 8.7
Contribution of Major Markets to East Asia's[a] Export Growth in Real Terms[b], 1965–88
(Per cent)

	Share					Contribution[c]				
	1965	1975	1985	1987	1988[d]	65–75	75–85	85–88	65–87	65–88
Japan	6.4	10.7	9.2	8.0	11.0	12.9	8.1	14.7	8.2	11.5
East Asia	23.9	32.5	33.6	32.1	33.7	36.8	34.4	33.8	33.1	34.7
North America	30.9	23.0	33.8	34.2	29.2	19.1	41.7	19.7	34.6	29.0
EEC 12	15.2	13.9	11.7	15.8	16.7	13.3	10.1	27.0	15.9	16.9
World	100.0	100.0	100.0	100.0	100.0	100.0	100.0	100.0	100.0	100.0

Notes: [a] Japan, Korea, China, Hong Kong and ASEAN. Taiwan is not included.

[b] the unit value index for exports from all Asian developing countries except Taiwan and China was used as a deflator. The 1987 and 1988 data were deflated by data available for the first three quarters of 1987.

[c] The increase in East Asian exports to each region as a proportion of the total increase in East Asian exports.

[d] The 1988 data are estimates of annual exports based on performance in the first quarter of 1988.

Sources: IMF, *Direction of Trade Statistics* (Washington D.C., various issues); UN, *Monthly Bulletin of Statistics* (New York, 1988).

significantly higher proportion of other East Asian economies' exports in the recent period of lower United States imports.

The mutual trading interests among Pacific countries, together with the strong commitment to trade-oriented development strategies among the developing countries in the region, provide a likely springboard for trade and other foreign economic policy measures not only to accommodate the trade and development needs of all the countries with the region but also to strengthen the global system of commitments to an open international trade regime.

IV Origins of the Pacific Free Trade Area Proposal

The growth of the East Asian economy and of Pacific economic interdependence, the shift of world economic power away from Europe and the Atlantic towards East Asia and the Pacific, and the changed status of Japan and the United States in world affairs have all encouraged suggestions for a new focus in dealings among Pacific economies (Crawford 1968, p.10).

Prominent in this discussion has been the notion of a developing community of interests in the Pacific and the recognition of advantages in closer Pacific economic co-operation; but the debate about what forms of institution-building might best serve the interests of Pacific countries in managing and further developing their already substantial economic interrelationship has, until recently, eschewed the idea of integration European-style. It is illuminating to recall the context in which the Pacific Free Trade Area (PAFTA) idea first emerged, and of its revival as a focus in trade diplomacy.

Although the growth of East Asian and Pacific economic interdependence did not originate in the establishment of formal regional institutional arrangements, two important elements in the nexus of political and commercial history in which this interdependence took place can be identified easily. The first is the role played by the GATT in post-war recovery and growth; the second is the dominance of the United States during this formative period.

The GATT-based trade regime grew out of the Atlantic Charter and the Mutual Aid Agreements of the wartime period (Finlayson and Zacher 1981) and served well the cause of reconstruction and liberalization of trade and economic activity for the first few decades or so after World War II. It provided the essentials of a global trade regime, far from comprehensive in its coverage of commodities or commercial interests (as some hoped the aborted plan for an International Trade Organization might have been), yet hugely supportive of trade expansion and world economic recovery and growth generally (Keohane and Nye 1977). This was critical to countries in East Asia and the Western Pacific, which were not immediate or direct beneficiaries under the initial rules and terms of GATT, but the GATT-based trading system also directed and limited trade and economic growth in some areas.

Second, the United States dominated the Pacific economy during that period. American leadership, regional as well as global, was comprehensive and hegemonic, combining military-strategic, political and economic interests. In this period the Pacific alliance against the Soviet bloc in the Cold War era was conceived and executed.

The GATT framework (and importantly Japan's eventual accommodation within it under the aegis of the United States) and the framework of the Pacific security alliances provided the underpinnings for the confident development of trading links within the East Asian and Pacific economy.

The idea of a community of Pacific countries associated in some form of regional arrangement began to emerge in the middle of the 1960s, principally in business and academic circles, and later, tentatively, in official quarters (Drysdale and Patrick 1979). The motive for the interest in this idea was the preservation of the opportunities for internationally oriented economic development, which had generated such spectacular results, against corrosive pressures generated by that growth itself, and against emergence of economic introversion in Europe associated with the entrenchment and expansion of the EEC.

At that time, as still now, the United States-Japan relationship was the most important in the Pacific region. But Australia and Japan were developing a quite significant bilateral economic relationship, which had grown out of commercial initiatives in the mid-1950s. In their subsequent reactions to the changing international economic environment, both countries moved to a closer involvement with each other. There is no better illustration of this than their response to the emergence of the EEC and the problems of global market access in the middle of the 1960s (Drysdale and Patrick 1979, pp.18–21).

Australia's response to the damaging effects of the European Common Agricultural Policy on the prospects for Australian economic growth based on the expansion of its traditional markets for agricultural exports was to intensify the development of new markets in Japan, and East Asia (Crawford and Okita 1976, pp.25–30). Japan's response to the emergence of a discriminatory bloc in Western Europe and increasing dependence on raw materials supplies from the region was to encourage closer economic relations with its main Pacific trading partners, and to pursue a line of commercial diplomacy designed to counter the effects of intensified European protectionism by developing an alignment of interests within the Pacific economy (Kojima 1971, Chapters 1, 3).[9]

The first detailed proposal for a Pacific regional economic association took the form of a free trade area scheme and emerged in Japan (Soesastro 1983, pp.3–53). The rationale advanced for institutional integration, involving discriminatory treatment in international trade, was based on an analysis of the effects of the formation of the European Economic Community on the Pacific five advanced industrial countries and on the relations between them and the developing countries of Asia and the Pacific (the "extended Pacific area") (Soesastro 1983, pp.3–53). The starting point in this argument was that "each time a shock was felt from outside the five Pacific countries, the necessity for closer Pacific integration was felt more seriously" (Soesastro 1983, pp.3–53; Kojima 1977, p.180).

The proposal for a Pacific Free Trade Area, consisting of the Pacific five as full members and incorporating East Asian developing as associate members enjoying non-reciprocated tariff concessions, was primarily a reaction to the establishment of the European Economic Community (Soesastro 1983, pp.28–31). The EEC was destined, it was felt, not only to have a huge impact on international trade and investment flows, but also on world economic power. The completion of the EEC's internal tariff elimination in 1968 added to fears of an increasingly inward looking and self-sufficient European bloc damaging to Pacific interests in global market access.[10] The logic of Pacific economic integration was urged in response to the threat of institutional integration in Europe and as a vehicle for realizing the potential of the East Asian and Pacific region. The completion of the Kennedy Round of negotiations in 1967 gave tactical point to the PAFTA proposal (Soesastro 1983, p.28).

The most important factor working against the earlier Pacific Free Trade Area proposal was the global interest in United States commercial diplomacy. The United States could not easily or sensibly participate in discriminatory regional trading arrangements through a grouping of either European or Pacific countries; this course would have been quite incompatible with its stature in world trade at that time, and contrary to the main thrust of its approach to international trade policy.[11] Moreover, the Pacific five included countries of disparate size and lacked the degree of integration required to make the dismantling of protective measures within the group politically or economically feasible (Arndt 1967, pp.271–76).

Nonetheless, the foreign economic policy interest which underlay the Pacific Free Trade Area proposal, although perhaps over-ambitious and of limited immediate policy relevance, contained the seeds of a useful approach to important problems which were emerging in the growing economic and other relations among the diverse economies and societies of the East Asian and Pacific region (Drysdale 1969, pp.321–42). The huge growth of trade, investment and aid relationships among the countries of East Asia and the Pacific was spawning not only opportunities but quite predictable policy problems that would be managed less and less well within established bilateral arrangements or by individual countries unilaterally. In this context the first exposure of a Pacific Free Trade Area proposal provided a useful impetus to the evaluation of other ideas directed towards the objectives of closer Pacific economic co-operation.

In the following two decades, Pacific economic co-operation interests came to focus heavily on building institutions that were functionally related to the economic interests of individual Pacific countries and to the region as a whole, and on the evaluation of support for an open global economic regime within which East Asian and Pacific countries could continue their economic expansion. In 1980, a meeting in Canberra saw the establishment of the Pacific Economic Co-operation Council (PECC) (Drysdale 1988). The PECC meetings, with the involvement of government officials, industry leaders, and people from the research community, have led to productive exchanges on trade policy issues. They were part of the intellectual background to an early call for a new round of multilateral trade negotiations in December 1983, and for consultations among the officials of several Western Pacific countries, in preparation for what became the Uruguay Round of trade negotiations.

Such mechanisms are evolving because an infrastructure of regional consultation and co-operation is necessary to make the development of Pacific positions practicable; because of the region's growing industrial might and economic interdependence; because reduction of policy uncertainties offers large potential gain through a stronger framework for regional economic relations; and because they assist the communication of the diverse policy objectives of very different countries and of smaller and weaker economic partners in the Pacific. Growing knowledge among Pacific countries of each other's institutions and policy practices strengthens the level of mutual confidence in national economic policies and reduces psychological and political barriers to the movement of commodities, capital and the relocation of production, all of which can serve to enhance international welfare.

V Free Trade Areas Resuscitated

In the contemporary international economic policy environment, serious challenges to East Asian development ambitions have again emerged in the area of trade policy. A characteristic of industrial transformation in East Asian countries is that their trade growth has required the taking over of market shares from established exporters, first in labour-intensive manufactured goods (as Japan did from Britain and Europe in the pre-war and post-war periods) and as the other newly industrializing countries of East Asia have done from Japan and in recent decades from one another (Garnaut and Anderson 1980; Drysdale 1988). It follows that arrangements that limit or discriminate against this type of trade growth and transformation would, by ossifying established trade shares, frustrate East Asian development ambitions, adversely affect Pacific trade interests and, thereby, limit the growth potential of the world economy.

The thrust of the GATT trade regime and other international institutions established after World War II was towards the establishment of an open trade regime which embodied, importantly, the principles of "non-discrimination", "predictability", "transparency" and "openness" (Dunn 1983, p.109; Crawford 1968, pp.127–76; Snape 1984, p.17). These principles steadily gained expression in successive GATT reviews and rounds of trade liberalization, in the unconditional most-favoured-nation rule, in the adoption of tariffs as the principal and "acceptable" form of trade protection, and in the "binding" of tariff rates to negotiated levels.[12] In applying these principles and rules, the architects of GATT sought to avoid the experience of trade restrictions, bilateralism and uncertainty of the interwar years and develop a confident global framework in which the benefits of trade liberalization would flow to all from the action of a relatively small number of major trading nations (Dunn 1983, Ch.5).

A trading system incorporating these principles and rules was of particular importance to smaller countries seeking economic growth through trade expansion. One of the great achievements of the United States and multilateral commercial diplomacy in the post-war period was undoubtedly the accommodation of Japan within the GATT most-favoured-nation trading framework, despite the initial application of Article XXXV permitting discrimination against Japan by many trading nations until the 1960s. Without appeal to GATT principles and the GATT framework, Japan would hardly have been able to achieve so smoothly its economic growth and trade expansion of the first few decades after the war. An open international market where trade discrimination is constrained by general adherence to the most-favoured-nation rule allows the accommodation of new and competitive suppliers, for whom trade is a central factor to economic growth and industrialization. And so, in the post-war period, the GATT regime has facilitated a major transformation in the geographic structure of world trade and the emergence of East Asia's economy. The main "external" influence on the trade policy interests of East Asian and Western Pacific countries continues to lie in the economic relationships of these countries with the United States. The United States is a major market for manufactured goods exports from the region. The Northeast Asian countries in particular are likely to see more value in trade liberalization movements if they include the United States. For its part, the United States has shown an increasing interest in the Western Pacific as the region has grown in importance, and the share of United States trade with the region has increased. Thus far, as is evident even in respect of Japan, the United States has tended to approach trade relations with particular East Asian countries in a case-by-case bilateral manner, the results of which have not always been consistent with most-favoured-nation principles.

In the lead-up to launching the new GATT round, the United States shifted towards a trade diplomacy based on the conditional most-favoured-nation approach, seeking "free trade area solutions" to its trade policy problems.[13] The agreement with Israel and the negotiation of a free trade arrangement with Canada were important targets in this policy approach (as well as the much-heralded Caribbean free trade arrangement). There seems to be strong interest in the United States for entering closer economic arrangements with Mexico, thus moving towards a North American free trade area. There are also suggestions at this time for some sort of "free trade area" association between the United States and Western Pacific countries (ASEAN, Australia and others). On the face of it, it seems that these United States suggestions are not aimed at the ultimate establishment of a Pacific free trade area but rather at setting up a bilateral dealing mechanism between the United States and some Western Pacific countries on a different footing from, and separate from, United States bilateral dealings with Japan. Whichever is the case, Western Pacific countries have been given reasons to consider a "free trade area" association in the Pacific.

VI Problems in the United States-Japan Relationship

For Pacific countries, the most important game-play in international trade diplomacy still revolves around the management of the economic relationship between the United States and Japan.[14] This is the most important relationship within the Pacific economy, and among the most important in the world. The way in which trade and commercial policies had come to be practised in the Pacific by the mid-1980s focused sharply on the serious imbalances between the United States and Japan and they were one motivation in the evaluation of a new free trade area approach to Pacific trade diplomacy.

Heightened tension in the management of the United States-Japan relationship in the first half of the 1980s resulted mainly from serious miscalculations in the macroeconomic policies of both countries, and the lack of effective macroeconomic policy co-ordination. This was a recurrent problem from the late 1960s, but extreme imbalances, focused on rising United States current account deficits and Japanese surpluses, emerged very rapidly between 1981 and 1985. The main adjustments for Japan and for the United States had to be on the macroeconomic front, and those adjustments were set in train, rather belatedly, after the Plaza Agreement of September 1985 forced the pace through the exchange-rate shift (Drysdale 1988, Ch.9).

These developments in the United States-Japan relationship were of some consequence for the shape of Pacific trade diplomacy. Both countries were diverted into attempts to resolve their global trade imbalances by action directed at each other (both negative and positive action: specific restrictions or surcharges; and bilateral market access arrangements). In the conduct of the United States-Japan relationship, specific trade issues came to dominate the policy approach. A related development, and danger for Western Pacific and other countries, was that Japan-targeting by the United States and the American obsession in Japan led both parties to negotiate bilateral deals that were damaging to third parties and to confidence in the whole trading system.

The cry of "specific reciprocity" as the guiding principle for trade and commercial policy became stronger and stronger in the United States over this period. "Specific reciprocity" (the careful equilibration of benefits in country-by-country and sector-by-sector settlements in which market-sharing arrangements are the goal and tit for tat is a legitimate strategy) is contrasted with the "uncertain benefits" of "diffuse reciprocity" (such as is embedded in the GATT system, under which multilateral negotiations and agreements foster a set of rules and norms in which reciprocity seeks an overall balancing of concessions).[15] "Strategic trade policy" and "fair trade" are the intellectual and political slogans heralding this new American policy environment.[16] In the 1980s, the Reagan Administration clung to the rhetoric of "diffuse reciprocity"; the political processes increasingly demanded the practice of "specific reciprocity". The political processes, and eventually the intellectual argument, targeted on Japan in justifying the retreat from support for a global regime based upon multilateral agreements and "diffuse reciprocity".[17]

In the negotiations preparatory to the extension of an international systemic public good, such as are involved in changes to the trade regime through a new GATT round, interplay between the interests of "specific reciprocity" (among the major groups of trading nations) and "diffuse reciprocity" (the application of generalized rules and norms of behaviour) is a natural if not essential ingredient (Keohane 1986, pp.19–27). The first step in the process addresses the "free rider" problem among the principal players, encouraging all of them to join in the exchange of concessions; the second delivers "stable, beneficial agreements in complex multilateral situations" involving domestic politics and international relations as well as economic interests (Keohane 1986, p.19).

Certainly Japan's role in trade liberalization and the negotiation of international settlements on other commercial policy, exchange rate and macroeconomic policy issues is a central element in Pacific economic policy, but it will only be supportive of broader Pacific policy objectives if it finally eschews "specific reciprocity" in dealings with the United States and does not neglect third country interests. The idea, with which Ambassador Mansfield has been associated, of a United States-Japan free trade area, is not therefore a sensible ultimate goal. The question in this context is whether third country interests are sufficiently encompassed within the Pacific to make attractive the idea of a broader Pacific free trade association. The short answer to that question must be that Japan's interests (as well as those of the newly industrializing countries of East Asia) now extend well beyond any group of Pacific countries that could readily or easily join a Pacific free trade area. The importance of the European relationship, the delicate development of interdependence with China, the emergence of the Soviet bloc and the opportunity for the emergence of Vietnam and the DPRK from their past isolation are only some of the factors that extend East Asia's "third country" interests and commitments to the multilateral trade and economic system.

VII Response to the Free Trade Area Proposals

One possible response to United States expressions of interest in special trade relations with various Western Pacific countries is to call for negotiations to establish a Pacific Free Trade Area, covering the United States, Canada, and some combination of economies from the Western Pacific.

Would such a response be helpful to the key strategic objectives we identified earlier: the shoring up of the system of imperfectly open trade in the Pacific that has facilitated rapid growth encompassing successively most of East Asia; the reduction of barriers to intra-Pacific trade; and the reduction of European barriers to Pacific trade?

A free trade area is more likely to bring net benefits the larger the economic size of the union envisaged. We have observed that the Pacific, as we have defined it, accounts for just under one half of world production of goods and services, and is likely to account for a higher proportion in future.

The Pacific countries are more important to each other's trade and potential trade than these output figures alone would suggest. The exceptionally high complementarity discussed earlier in the paper, and the economic advantages of intense Western Pacific trade that derive from location, each point to an increased likelihood that a Pacific Free Trade Area would generate net benefits for its members and, though less powerfully, for the world as a whole.

We have observed that barriers to trade in Pacific countries are highest in precisely those commodities within which the comparative advantage of other Pacific countries is strongest: protection in Japan, Taiwan and South Korea against agricultural exports from Australasia and North America; protection in Australasia and North America against labour-intensive exports from China, the Asian NIEs and other ASEAN countries, and against exports of a range of more capital-intensive standard technology products, especially motor vehicles, from Japan and the Asian NIEs. This increases the likelihood of net gains from a Pacific Free Trade Area that is not subject to important exemptions.

The last qualification is important. The reality of free trade areas and customs unions in practice is that exceptions have been important at least in their early years; and where they have not, the establishment of the area has been associated with increased barriers to trade with the rest of the world. This outcome is driven by an important asymmetry in the political economy of protection policy, between the highly focused opposition to trade creation by established interests in protected industries, together with the highly focused support of established interests in trade diversion on the one hand, and the diffuse beneficiaries from trade creation on the other (Anderson and Garnaut 1987, Ch.4). Hence the tendencies to higher protection against the rest of the world that can be observed early in the lives of the United States, Canadian, Australian and European customs unions, and the proliferation of exceptions early in the lives of the Australia-New Zealand and United States-Canada Free Trade Areas.

One would be blind to the realities of the political economy of protection to ignore the likelihood that, in a Pacific Free Trade Area, the process of negotiation and compromise would favour trade diversion over trade creation.

Neither can we presume that all Pacific countries would seek to participate in negotiations to establish a free trade area. China, with its partly reformed prices system, is not now in a position to accept the obligations of participation in a "clean" free trade area. It would be possible in principle to negotiate a range of commitments to open trade by China that led in the direction of more open and, perhaps free trade. But the presence of special rules to govern China's trade relations with the Pacific would invite the proliferation of commitments short of free trade by other participants, especially (but not only) in developing countries. Yet to exclude China would carry considerable costs. It could retard China's progress towards more open trade relations, thus reducing the chances of ultimate success in the whole modernization programme. Trade diversion from China within a smaller Pacific Free Trade Area would generate tensions and retaliation that would carry costs of their own. And if China continued to grow strongly despite these new obstacles, over time a progressively smaller proportion of opportunities for profitable intra-Pacific trade would be covered by the Free Trade Area, thus weakening the presumption of net benefits for members and the world as a whole.

Nor is it likely that the ASEAN countries would accept membership of a clean free trade area. Governments in Indonesia, the Philippines, Malaysia and even Thailand have all compromised heavily in implementing trade liberalization programmes over the past decade (Findlay and Garnaut 1986, pp.271–73). Attempts at intra-ASEAN liberalization have yielded much more trade diversion than trade creation. Despite the attraction of open access to North American and Australasian markets it is unlikely that the ASEAN states would agree to participate fully. To exclude ASEAN and to expose its members to trade diversion in favour of other Pacific economies would reduce the gains from Pacific integration, and set back the hesitant process of trade liberalization in the ASEAN economies themselves. To welcome ASEAN membership on a non-reciprocal or incompletely reciprocal basis would invite pressures elsewhere for the proliferation of exceptions.

We defined our first objective as the preservation of the relatively but imperfectly open trading environment that had supported the productive extension of rapid growth in East Asia in recent decades. This objective seems to us to rule out embarking on an integration process that runs a severe risk of setting back severely the prospects for internationally oriented growth in China and the ASEAN states.

Now let us presume for analytic purposes that it were possible to wave a magic diplomatic wand and embark on a process of negotiation that delivers a clean and comprehensive Pacific Free Trade Area. Would such a process help or hinder the reduction of barriers to trade between Pacific countries and trading partners in the rest of the world?

The process of establishment of a Pacific Free Trade Area would require a huge concentration of political and administrative effort in all member countries. This would inevitably divert attention from wider trade policy objectives in the international system.

This effort would follow perceptions of failure in the Uruguay Round of trade negotiations and disillusionment with the multilateral trading system. But the fact of disappointment with the GATT-based system would not in itself demonstrate that an imperfect system of wider international trading relations could not get worse.

It is not clear to us how a commitment to a Pacific Free Trade Area, involving substantial trade diversion away from the rest of the world in the best of scenarios, would facilitate the negotiations of lower trade barriers with the European Communities. It is possible that the threat of such developments would focus

European governments more clearly on the need for success in the Uruguay Round. But action to implement this threat would have the effect of, at best, suspending progress on the negotiation of reciprocal liberalization with Europe during a long transitional process.

Similarly, the diversion of trade policy-making resources into the development of PAFTA, and the diversion of trade from the rest of the world, would weaken the region's capacity to respond to early stirrings of interest in internationally oriented development in the Soviet Union and Indochina, and the tentative signs of possible future stirrings in the DPRK that can be read into recent statements on Korea from the Soviet Union. For the foreseeable future, the expansion of trade relations between the Pacific countries and these centrally planned economies is of minor importance in narrowly economic terms. But it would be foolish to diminish the potential for reduction in political tension and the threat of war, and eventually reduction in military expenditure, that would over time be associated with constructive Pacific responses to these centrally planned economies' interest in closer economic relations.

The United States at least would be mindful of Mexican and other Latin American interests in the process of Pacific integration. The accommodation of these interests would further increase the likelihood of special arrangements and exceptions within PAFTA.

It may seem that the liberalization of access to trade in services appears more likely to be susceptible to treatment under the aegis of the "free trade area" approach. The obstacles to international competition in services do not arise mainly through fiscal mechanisms as they do with tariffs on commodities. They take the form of government monopoly of services (communications); government controls on entry or capacity (aviation); prescriptions of qualifications for entry (professional services); or rules on domestic content (media). Some of the restrictions involve international agreements on rights or conditions of operation. These issues may appear easier to press through arrangements such as the Australia-New Zealand Closer Economic Relations Trade Agreement. However, although their multilateral negotiation may be difficult at this point, they are not likely to be treated easily within the framework of a Pacific Free Trade Area (as United States-Canada experience attests). Indeed, the complexities of service trade liberalization would seem equally amendable to negotiation within the framework of broader most-favoured-nation type trade and commerce agreements, alongside commodity trade issues.

We conclude that efforts to establish a Pacific Free Trade Area are not consistent with Pacific countries' interests in more effective movement towards global trade liberalization. Discriminatory trade arrangements in the Pacific region, and discriminatory treatment of Japan by the United States and other Western Pacific countries, or of other Western Pacific countries by Japan and the United States, are inconsistent with East Asian and Pacific trade policy interests and are likely to damage the growth of other countries in the region. If, on the other hand, the "free trade area" suggestion were not intended to involve trade discrimination within the Pacific, it may provide an impetus for accelerating movement towards liberalization on a most-favoured-nation basis, both in the region and more broadly.

The important requirement in such discussions would be to avoid any acceptance of the discrimination against non-Pacific countries implied by the term "free trade area", and to work to find areas of reciprocal concession that can be offered on a most-favoured-nation basis. But how can we reconcile this approach with recent tendencies in United States trade policy and, more broadly, with the reduced willingness of the United States to continue to provide liberal leadership to the multilateral trading system?

·VIII The Diminished Hegemon

The diminished relative position of the United States in the Pacific and world economies is an inevitable result of the success of American international economic policy in the post-war period.

The United States has prospered exceptionally in the liberal trading system of which it was the chief sponsor. And this same system has sponsored more rapid growth in smaller and initially much poorer American allies and trading partners as they have utilized opportunities for expanding gains from trade. This is exactly what a *priori* analysis would have led us to expect if we had known that the post-war mechanisms were going to work well. Yet instead of self-congratulation in the United States, we see recrimination and the adoption of attitudes and policies that threaten to undermine the liberal international system.

Some analysts have sought the explanation for the changed United States approach in a theory of the hegemonic leader in the supply of an international public good; the open, multilateral trading system. As by far the largest country in the early post-war system, and by implication the largest beneficiary of it, the United States needed and was prepared to play a leadership role in supplying the "public good", while letting "free riders" in Europe, Australasia, Japan and the developing countries escape the burden of accepting symmetric market-access obligations.[18] But the relative decline of the United States in world production and trade in the subsequent decades has diminished United States preparedness to carry the costs of leadership. Restoration of the health of the system requires the emergence of a new hegemon, willing and able to carry these costs. But there is none in sight.

There is a problem for an economist in this line of analysis. The required leadership, that is, maintaining an open system, may carry some adjustment costs, but conveys overall a benefit, presuming that the hegemony does not so dominate world markets that a diminution of the extent of its trade can improve its terms of trade sufficiently to outweigh the allocative costs of reduced specialization. In circumstances of hegemonic decline, the expectations of the leader gaining from free trade, even if its trading partners impose protection, are even larger, since variations in its own level of trade will be even less influential in determining relative prices. Symmetrically, the small country's imposition of barriers to trade, far from being a "free ride", imposes costs that, if anything, are greatest when its relative size is least.

Bhagwati (1988) has sought to rationalize observed tendencies in the international system by supposing that the United States earlier was acting as the leader in a different sense by permitting "justifiable asymmetries" of obligations on a temporary basis. As the temporary circumstances ended, with recovery in Europe and growth in the Western Pacific, the United States demanded reciprocity of access.

Again, there are problems with this logic if a rationale is sought in the calculation of national economic interest.

There are, however, two possible ways in which the United States might rationally have been pursuing national interest. First, the introduction of distortions into trade, to the cost of itself and its partners in the international system, might be rationally calculated to force partners to drop trade distortions of their own. This is the expressed objective of the massive retaliation against European agricultural subsidies through the United States' export enhancement programme.[19] It is incidental to this argument that the retaliatory instruments chosen by the United States imposed proportionately higher costs on innocent bystanders. The key test of rationality is whether the retaliation was well judged to force liberalization elsewhere. If the realities deny good prospects for such a response in Europe, the retaliation can only damage United States interests. Second, the descent into bilateralism seems to have had some success in enhancing United States interests at the expense of third parties through trade diversion. The United States has been able to pursue this approach in agriculture, where protection is commonly provided by administered import quotas which may be allocated to discriminate between suppliers. This might convey a narrow and short-term benefit to the United States alone, but this benefit would be offset to some extent by the indirect cost to the United States of losses borne by other allies and trading partners.

This has been important recently in United States bilateral initiatives towards increasing American shares of East Asian commodity markets. An important case in point concerns the Japanese beef trade. In the minerals trade, coal markets have been affected in a similar but lesser way through different mechanisms. In response to demands by the United States for greater access to the Japanese market, beef import restrictions were altered to allow more United States imports, but this has been at the expense of third countries, particularly Australia. In the four years to 1983, the United States share in the volume of Japanese beef and offal imports rose from 31 per cent to 44 per cent, while the Australian share fell from 62 per cent to 49 per cent. The total import volume rose by less than 10 per cent during the period (Anderson and Hayami 1986). This policy approach was turned around in the settlement with Japan in July 1988, when that country delivered reform of its beef trade system consistently with the important GATT principles of "transparency" and "non-discrimination".

Both in the "massive retaliation" against European subsidies and in the bilateral initiatives, any case for action in the United States' narrow national interest would have been as strong in earlier times as in recent years. It is not obvious how the relative decline of the United States in world production and trade would have strengthened the economic case for action in recent times.

The key to understanding the new United States attitudes to the international trading system lies outside anything that is happening mainly in that system itself, namely in the polity's incapacity to come to grips with profound macroeconomic imbalances. Other countries' protection policies are blamed for a payments imbalance that has its origins largely in domestic budgetary policy. The problem for other countries in managing the United States' challenge to the liberal system is that large-scale trade liberalization in East Asia and Europe is incapable of contributing in a major way to curing the United States current accounts problems. There would seem to be no reliable prospect for addressing current international trade tensions independently of United States progress in moderating domestic demand, in pursuit of reduced imbalance in current external payments.

This is where hegemonic decline may be important. The United States polity, wounded by macroeconomic difficulties, has lost tolerance for the weaknesses in the trade policy performance of others, independently of rationally calculated national advantage. The increase in relative size and strength of others is important principally for its effects on political reactions at all levels in the United States.

It is a dangerous time to take risks and liberties with the multilateral system.

IX A Pacific Approach to Liberalization

How then can the United States' partners in the Pacific respond to these powerful new currents in trade policy consistently with non-discriminatory liberalization?

Realization of the fragility of the system provides strong grounds to work towards success in the Uruguay Round. The United States' administration and wider polity is likely to judge success first of all in terms of progress on agriculture. The European Communities,

Japan and also Western Pacific developing countries would be wise to calculate carefully the cost of inadequate movement on agriculture, beyond the usual cost of foregone gains from trade.

Disappointing progress in the GATT Round will herald a highly dangerous period for the international trading system.

This will be a time for re-channelling interests in a Pacific Free Trade Area into renewed regionally based efforts to strengthen the multilateral system.

The strategic problem in pursuing discussions under the "free trade area" umbrella, will be to maintain a focus on non-discrimination and to find areas of reciprocal concessions which are capable of sustaining United States interest in the discussions. From the viewpoint of Western Pacific countries, the most important concessions by the United States would relate to access to the United States markets for manufactured goods in which East Asian countries are most competitive.

For the United States to extend such concessions on a most-favoured-nation basis would not, with the exception of steel, have a strong impact on United States-Europe trade. The areas of greatest Japanese competitiveness do not now coincide closely with European competitiveness in the United States market. In fact, initial United States concessions to Japan could simply consist of the removal of trade arrangements such as "voluntary export restraints" which discriminate against Japanese goods. However, concessions relevant to East Asian developing countries would affect United States trade with Latin America if offered on a most-favoured-nation basis. For this reason it would be sensible for the United States to engage Latin American countries in the process of reciprocation alongside Pacific discussions.

The main areas of concession that could be offered to the United States by Western Pacific countries are agricultural trade liberalization and liberalization of access to trade in services. The involvement of the United States in trade negotiations would make significant progress in agriculture more feasible, because of United States' interest in that area and because of the significance for Northeast Asian countries of the concessions that the United States would be able to offer in exchange.

Western Pacific developing countries would find advantage in increased access for labour-intensive manufactures, and more secure access for more capital-intensive standard technology manufactures in developed country markets.

Although the United States may have benefited from its country-by-country bilateral bargaining over access to East Asian commodity markets in the past, the benefits have been severely limited by the quantitative restrictions on overall agricultural trade. Movement towards more liberal agricultural trade would benefit Australasia, for example, relative to the United States by removing present discrimination, but would yield substantially greater gains to all agricultural exporters (including the United States) than have been achieved in existing bilateral dealings. Hence, Australia's initiative in forming the "Cairns Group" of efficient agricultural exporters has sought to engage the United States and other agricultural exporters in the negotiation of a more general and phased liberalization of the agricultural trading system (Australian National Pacific Cooperation Committee 1987, p.9; Stoekel and Cuthbertson 1987, Ch.2).

The approach suggested here draws its prospects for success from the tendency for barriers to intra-Pacific trade to be highest in commodities and markets in which other Pacific economies are competitive suppliers. The incentive for participation, beyond realization that the liberal trading system is in peril, is the opportunity to shape the agenda. The non-discriminatory nature of concessions avoids carrying the high costs of exclusions of the kind involved in PAFTA. China and the ASEAN countries need not be excluded by their incapacity to make comprehensive commitments to intra-Pacific free trade, so long as they are able to offer liberalization that contributes substantially to trade expansion. The "Pacific Round" would be entered at a time of crisis, and the developed countries and NIEs would be aware of the high consequences of failure to make substantial progress.

There would remain the problem of resentment in the United States polity of any "free ride" for European agriculture. There would be pressures for the United States to take its "massive retaliation" to a conclusion alongside the Pacific Round.

A much better strategy, should the European Community persist in current positions, may be to regionalize the retaliation and its costs in the context of the Pacific Round.

The fiscal burden could be shared by the developed countries, or by countries with per capita income above a specified level. The burden sharing would be fiscally and psychologically helpful in the United States. The fiscal commitments would be greatly unwelcome elsewhere in this region, but would need to be weighed against the benefits of strengthening the multilateral system and of genuine liberalization within that system. In Japan, they would need to be judged alongside other politically more difficult pressures for "burden sharing" with the United States. In Canada, Australia and New Zealand, they would be partly compensated by the alleviation of what has been in recent years a major sectoral problem, generated by the United States' unilateral implementation of the export enhancement programme. In the current fiscal circumstances of the United States, regional burden sharing, especially the participation of Japan, would substantially enhance the credibility of the retaliation. Hopefully such retaliation would never actually be required.

The central concept of a regional round of negotiations directed towards multilateral concessions, but focused on issues of high regional interest, has been discussed from time to time over the past decade. It only ever did, and still only does, make sense as a complement to the primary goal of a successful GATT Round. Its feasibility has been enhanced in recent years by the practice of regional co-operation in a wide range of trade policy matters, including preparation for the Uruguay Round.[20]

It seems to us that a response to failure in the Uruguay Round along these lines would hold out rather better prospects than PAFTA for holding the line on erosion of the multilateral system, promoting intra-Pacific liberalization, and securing progress on reduction of barriers to trade between Europe and the Pacific.

Notes

The authors gratefully acknowledge the assistance of Jeremy Whitham, Prue Phillips, Diana Elias, David Lawson, James Jorden and Elyse Tanoye in preparing data and gathering background information and also Kim Lan Ngo and Minni Reis for wordprocessing.

1. Richard Cooper (1974, pp.2–4) makes the useful distinction between "market" and "institutional" integration.
2. These data rely on World Bank (1987), United Nations (various issues), and Council for Economic Planning Development (1987). Data for centrally planned economies are net of material product. These are the standard measures of GDP used by the World Bank and other international agencies. We are aware that they do not provide perfect measures of the relative output of goods and services in different economic systems. (See Summers and Heston 1984.) When adjustments have been attempted for measurement imperfections, they have had the effect of substantially raising East Asia's share of world GDP, especially because they ascribe much higher production to China.
3. For an approach to the application of the theory of changing comparative advantage in East Asia, see Garnaut and Anderson (1980).
4. For example, 18.2 per cent for United States textiles, and 10.6 per cent for hides and leather (General Agreement on Tariffs and Trade 1980).
5. These data exclude petroleum products. They are unweighted average tariffs calculated using 1987 data from local tariff schedules.
6. It is to be hoped that recent discussion of dumping issues with Korea does not lead to the marring of this good record.
7. This issue has been traversed, somewhat inconclusively, in recent contributions from Lawrence (1987, pp.517–54), and from Saxonhouse and Stern (1988); for a good review of the discussion, see Takeuchi (1988).
8. The estimates in Pangestu and Boediono (1986) exclude rice milling and sugar refining.

9. For a review of the context of these developments, see Arndt (1987, p.79f).
10. The original contribution to this discussion was made in Kojima and Kurimoto (1966, pp.93–134). Under the Foreign Ministry of Takeo Miki in Japan, the first Pacific Trade and Development Conference was organized at the Japan Economic Research Center, Tokyo, January 1968, to evaluate Kojima's proposal. See Drysdale (1984).
11. Parts of the argument in this section are elaborated in and drawn from Drysdale (1988, pp.207–25).
12. Snape (1984) notes that Harry Johnson says of non-discrimination, "That principle has absolutely nothing to recommend it on grounds of either economic policy or the realities of international commercial diplomacy", but nevertheless endorses it as the best principle available (Johnson 1976, pp.30–31).
13. For background to this policy approach, see Hay and Sulzenko (1982); Cline (1982); Wonnacott (1984); Bhagwati and Irwin (1987); and Snape (1988).
14. Among the best reviews of developments in the United States-Japan relationship during this period is Patrick (1987).
15. Keohane (1986, p.1027) sets out the distinction between "specific" and "diffuse" reciprocity most clearly. Krasner (1986, pp.787–806) takes up the distinction to rationalize a strategy of "specific reciprocity" in United States dealings with Japan.
16. Grossman and Richardson (1985, pp.1–34) provide a recent review of this literature. Among the more important contributions in the international relations literature that have encouraged this interest is by Axelrod (1983).
17. Krasner (1986, p.289), for example, sees Japan as an economy which "defies external penetration .... Japanese institutions, both public and private, are linked in a dense network of reciprocal obligations" and he goes on to say that "it is extremely difficult for new actors to pierce this network ..." He concludes that: "If domestic-political-economic structures vary, then similar universal rules such as those codified in the GATT, can have very different behavioural outcomes. Tariff reductions in a market-oriented system like the United States will offer more opportunities to foreign producers than similar reductions in Japan, because buyers are more likely to consider only the costs and benefits of a specific transaction rather than to also incorporate assessments about past and future relationships with prospective suppliers. Diffuse reciprocity will not work even in the absence of conscious efforts at exploitation by the Japanese. The differences between the domestic structures of these two states guarantees [sic] that a universal open system based upon diffuse reciprocity will leave the United States with the 'sucker's payoff'".
18. For a discussion of this idea, see Bhagwati (1988, Ch.3[D]).
19. Colleagues at a seminar that one of the authors (Garnaut) gave recently at the East Asian Institute of Columbia University pointed to the parallel between the Reagan Administration's export enhancement programme, directed at the European Communities, and the military build-up, directed at the Soviet

Union. At high short-term costs to the United States, these commitments imposed costs on adversaries to provide a congenial environment for negotiations on reciprocal disarmament. The effectiveness of each strategy depends on a series of find judgments.

20. See Garnaut (1981, pp.14–30). When the Australian Prime Minister, R. J. L. Hawke, called for a new round of multilateral trade negotiation in a speech in Bangkok in December 1983, he referred to a regional round along the lines suggested here as a fallback should efforts to launch and to implement a new round fail.

9
AUSTRALIA IN THE WESTERN PACIFIC ECONOMY

The Western Pacific region comprises thirteen significant trading economies which now provide the greater part of the annual expansion of each other's trading opportunities. Although the Western Pacific economies contribute only about one-sixth of total world trade, almost all of them transact about one-half of their foreign trade with other Western Pacific economies. There is similarly high intensity of trade within and between each of the three subregions of the Western Pacific: Northeast Asia, ASEAN, and the Southwest Pacific. High intensity of trade within the Western Pacific region has grown out of geographic proximity and common exclusion from the intense trading relationship amongst the industrial economies of North America and Europe.

This regional concentration of trade has aided the export

This chapter is extracted from a paper at a meeting of the Victorian Branch of the Economic Society of Australia in August 1980. The extract was amongst the background papers at the inaugural Pacific Economic Co-operation Council meeting at the Australian National University in September 1980. The full paper was published as Garnaut (1981).

growth of each of the Western Pacific economies because the region as a whole has enjoyed much stronger economic growth than the rest of the world throughout the period since the mid-1960s. The Western Pacific share of total exports of the world's market economies grew steadily, from 11.3 per cent in 1963 to 12.6 per cent in 1968, 15.4 per cent in 1973 and 16.2 per cent by 1977. At first this reflected mainly the dynamism of the Northeast Asian market economies, both Japan and the developing countries Hong Kong, South Korea and Taiwan. But the ASEAN countries made a substantial contribution to the expansion in the Western Pacific region's share in world trade from about 1968, and more particularly after 1973 when the advanced industrial countries went into their transition to slower growth.

All of the Northeast Asian and Southeast Asian economies have entered the world economy as exporters of industrial raw materials and foodstuffs — even Japan in pre-war years and South Korea and Taiwan until the early 1960s. In the most natural resource-poor countries, notably Japan, Hong Kong, South Korea, Taiwan and Singapore, there was a rapid switch to exporting mainly manufactures, with heavy reliance on a few labour-intensive manufactured exports. The switch has come more slowly, at a time when real wages were much higher, and with less reliance on a few simple labour-intensive manufactures, in Malaysia and the Southwest Pacific, where there is higher *per capita* endowment of natural resources.

Continued economic growth and capital accumulation have tended to absorb all surplus labour from agriculture into urban industry, whereupon real wages have begun to rise and comparative advantage has tended to shift from simple labour-intensive manufactures to more complex and capital-intensive manufactures. This turning-point in economic development occurred in the early 1960s in Japan and the early 1970s in South Korea, Taiwan and Singapore. This graduation of the more advanced East Asian countries out of strong specialization in the export of labour-intensive manufactures has made way in world markets for others.

Amongst the technologically simple and labour-intensive manufactures which have been the mainstays of all of the Northeast and Southeast Asian economies, textiles, clothing and footwear have been pre-eminent. These commodities contributed about one-quarter of Japan's total manufactured exports in the early 1960s, and the share fell steadily every year to a low of 4.5 per cent in 1979. Over the same period, the share of textiles, clothing and footwear in Japanese imports of manufactures grew rapidly, from only 3.1 per cent in 1963 to a peak of 17.8 per cent in the boom year 1973, before falling back in the mid-1970s recession and rising again to 17.5 per cent in 1979. Textiles, clothing and footwear contributed over 60 per cent of Hong Kong manufactured exports in the early 1960s and about 46 per cent in 1979. These commodities contributed over one-half of South Korea's manufactured exports through the period from the mid-1960s until the early 1970s when high growth was being entrenched, and still represents over 40 per cent. In Taiwan, the equivalent ratio was over 40 per cent from 1968 to 1973 and it remains over one-third. Textiles, clothing and footwear have represented between one-third and one-half of the rapidly expanding manufactured exports from Thailand since the early 1970s. They contributed one-quarter of Indonesia's greatly increased manufactured exports in 1979 and are likely to increase in relative importance over the next few years if the current impetus to export-oriented manufacturing growth is maintained in that country. Recently announced shifts in emphasis in the modernization drive of the People's Republic of China suggest that simple labour-intensive commodities will play a major role in the export expansion of that country in the immediate future.

The liberal international trading system of the 1960s and early 1970s provided a highly favourable environment for the rapid industrialization of Northeast Asia and for the beginnings of manufactured export expansion in the ASEAN countries. It allowed exports from this region to expand greatly their share of consumption of labour-intensive manufactures in the advanced industrial countries. It facilitated Japan's transition into export specialization in standard technology capital-intensive commodities through the 1960s, and the beginnings of the transition in South Korea, Taiwan and Singapore in the early 1970s.

But from the onset of worldwide recession in 1974, doubts have been raised about whether the international trading environment can sustain continued rapid industrialization in the Western Pacific based on the dynamism of newly industrializing countries specializing in the export of labour-intensive manufactures. Not only did total demand for manufactures in the advanced industrial countries grow much more slowly from 1974, but an upsurge in protectionist sentiment throughout the world led to much slower growth in the proportion of domestic consumption of labour-intensive manufactures supplied by imports.

Nowhere were these new tendencies more apparent than in Australia. Total Australian imports of textiles, clothing and footwear were valued at US$1,227 million in 1974, but the imposition of import quotas in that year and their subsequent intensification led to a sharp decline, so that the dollar value of US$1,174 million in 1977 was still substantially below the 1974 peak. The proportion of Australian domestic consumption of textiles, clothing and footwear supplied by imports declined from 27 per cent to 26 per cent over the same period. Nevertheless, increasing competitiveness of Northeast and Southeast Asian developing countries meant that they were able to increase their share of the Australian market in the face of a declining total share of imports.

The most interesting feature of the "new protectionism" in Australia was that it was heavily focused precisely on those commodities which were the mainstays of export growth in the newly industrializing Western Pacific countries. The average effective rate of protection for manufactured goods was 36 per cent from 1968–69 to 1972–73. It fell sharply to 27 per cent in 1973–74 as a result of the 25 per cent across-the-board tariff cut of July 1973. It has since drifted further downwards to 25 per cent in 1977–78. Over the same period, average effective protection against imports of the main developing country products has increased dramatically: for textiles, from 45 per cent in 1972–73 to 35 per cent in 1973–74 and 56 per cent in 1977–78; and for clothing and footwear from 88 per cent in 1972–73 to 64 per cent in 1973–74 and 149 per cent in 1977–78. The greatly increased Australian protection for the main developing country exports has been entrenched by the success of industry lobbies in securing forward commitments on maintaining domestic production in the run up to the 1977 election, and in 1980 in the shadow of another election.

The Australian case is only one example of a worldwide phenomenon, which threatens to remove the basis of the strong export-oriented industrialization of Northeast and Southeast Asian industrialization. This is occurring at the same time as the demographic giants of Northeast and Southeast Asia, the People's Republic of China and Indonesia, have been expressing an interest in following, and taking the first steps, along the path of rapid industrialization based on exports of labour-intensive manufactures.

The export-oriented industrialization of Northeast and Southeast Asia has so far been resilient to the increased protection in advanced industrial countries since 1974. The main reason for this has been the rapid transformation of Japan's foreign trade specialization over this period, from being the largest net exporter of textiles, clothing and footwear, to having zero net exports in 1979. Developing countries in the region have increased exports by selling to Japan, and by taking over markets in third countries formerly supplied by Japan. Japan can continue to provide important opportunities for exports from Northeast and Southeast Asian developing countries as it emerges as a major net importer of labour-intensive manufactures. The Japanese adjustment has itself been facilitated by the maintenance of a favourable international environment for exports of more technologically complex and capital-intensive commodities. But this environment is itself under stronger threat, at least in Europe and North America, in the recession that has followed the 1978–79 oil crises. Japanese willingness to adjust would also be weakened by any deceleration of economic growth in other Western Pacific countries.

The gains to all countries from economic growth based on exploitation of comparative advantage in international trade are attested clearly by the experience of the past two decades. And yet it is becoming increasingly apparent that appeals to the national advantage in unilaterally pursuing liberal trade policies have been ineffective in maintaining a willingness to accept structural adjustment in the light of changing comparative advantage in the Western Pacific region. Vested interests in established economic structures have always applied pressure to governments to introduce protectionist policies. In the post-1974 environment of reduced confidence in the open international trading system, doubts about continued access to export markets have reduced resistance to domestic protectionist pressures in most Western Pacific countries.

While appeals to national advantage in unilateral pursuit of liberal trade policies have not been effective, neither do the multilateral trade arrangements through GATT hold out much hope. The Tokyo Round has confirmed that protection against the export staples of the Southwest Pacific and developing Northeast and Southeast Asia — agricultural products and textiles, clothing and footwear — are "exceptions" to the general aim to maintain a liberal international trading system.

There must be some hope that negotiations on market access on a regional basis, among Western Pacific countries, could yield the gains that unilateral and multilateral mechanisms have failed to deliver. The high regional shares of each Western Pacific country's foreign trade would seem to facilitate regional trade bargaining.

Regional negotiations could aim to liberalize trade, or to seek assurances that there would be no increases in protection in commodities in which Western Pacific countries are the major suppliers to the region. Concessions could then be given on a most-favoured-nation basis. The choice of commodities would ensure that the opportunities that were provided for export expansion were available mainly to participants in the regional trade negotiations.

Australia's strongest interests in such regional negotiations would lie in obtaining improved access to the Japanese market and continued favourable access to Southeast and Northeast Asian developing country markets, for foodstuffs and processed metals. These industries are amongst Australia's most productive, and they have been exceptionally vulnerable to protectionist pressures as incomes have grown in the countries that are now industrialized. Australia would seek to avoid the danger that the newly industrialized countries — to their own as well as Australia's cost — would follow in the footsteps of Europe, Japan, and to a lesser extent the United States, in extending high protection to domestic food and metals production. Other Southwest Pacific countries would have much to gain from these same assurances — New Zealand especially on foodstuffs, and Papua New Guinea especially on metals.

The newly industrializing countries would obviously be seeking assurances on access to markets for labour-intensive manufactures — from the countries like South Korea that had prospects of graduating out of being major net exporters of these commodities as well as from the region's advanced industrial economies. Japan might be especially interested in market access for motor vehicles and some high technology manufactures. There is ample scope for agreement on a set of assurances on market access that held out the prospect of substantial net gains for all participants.

The negotiations could be open-ended around a core of Western Pacific countries, with invitations to participate being extended to other countries that were willing to make offers on market access that were judged to be meaningful by the convening governments.

The expectation, or at least the hope, would be that the political economy of trade policy in each Western Pacific country could accommodate import policy assurances and concessions more easily when they were linked by international agreement to opportunities for further expansion of the country's most productive industries. Vested interests in export expansion would be brought into direct conflict, and so help to balance, vested interests in protection. And the reciprocal assurances on market access would reduce anxiety within each of the Western Pacific polities that growth based on strong foreign trade specialization might be undermined at some future time by changes in trade policy abroad.

REFERENCES

Akrasanee, Narongchai and Juanjai Ajanant. 1986. "Thailand: Manufacturing Industry, Protection Issues and Empirical Studies". In Christopher Findlay and Ross Garnaut, eds., *The Political Economy of Manufacturing Protection: Experiences of ASEAN and Australia*. Sydney: Allen & Unwin.

Anderson, Kym and Yujiro Hayami, eds. 1986. *The Political Economy of Agricultural Protection: East Asia in International Perspective*. Sydney: Allen & Unwin.

—— and Ross Garnaut. 1987. *Australian Protection: Extent, Causes and Effects*. Sydney and Boston: Allen & Unwin.

APEC (Asia-Pacific Economic Co-operation Ministerial Meeting). 1992. "Joint Statement and Bangkok Declaration on Asia-Pacific Economic Co-operation Institutional Arrangements", September. Reprinted in *ASEAN Economic Bulletin* 9, no.2 (November 1992).

—— (Asia-Pacific Economic Co-operation Ministerial Meeting). 1993. "Declaration of APEC Ministers on the Uruguay Round", November. Reprinted in *ASEAN Economic Bulletin* 10, no. 3 (March 1994).

Arndt, H.W. 1967. "PAFTA: An Australian Assessment". *Intereconomics* 10.

—— 1987. *Economic Development*. Chicago: Chicago University Press.

――― and R.M. Sundrum. 1975. "Regional Price Disparities". *Bulletin of Indonesian Economic Studies* 11, no.2 (July).

Asia-Pacific Economics Group. 1996. *Asia-Pacific Profiles 1996*. Canberra: Australian National University.

Australian National Pacific Cooperation Committee. 1987. *Australia and Pacific Cooperation*. Second Report of the Australian National Pacific Cooperation Committee, Canberra.

Axelrod, Robert. 1983. *The Evolution of Cooperation*. New York: Basic Books.

Bergsten, C. Fred. 1994. "APEC and the World Economy: A Force for Worldwide Liberalization". *Foreign Affairs* 73, no.3 (May–June): 20–26.

Bhagwati, Jagdish. 1988. *Protectionism*. Boston: MIT Press.

――― and Douglas A. Irwin. 1987. "The Return of the Reciprocitarians: US Trade Policy Trade". *The World Economy* 10, no.2.

――― and Patrick H.T. eds. 1991. *Aggressive Unilateralism: American Trade Policy & the World Trading System*. Ann Arbor: University of Michigan Press.

Cline, William. 1982. "'Reciprocity': A New Approach to World Trade Policy?" *Policy Analyses in International Economics* 2 (Washington D.C.: Institute for International Economics).

Cooper, R. 1974. "Worldwide Versus Regional Integration: Is There an Optimal Size of the Integrated Area". *Yale Economic Growth Centre Discussion Paper*, no.220 (November).

Corden, W.M. 1971. *The Theory of Protection*. Oxford: Clarendon Press.

―――. 1974. *Trade Policy and Economic Welfare*. Oxford: The Clarendon Press.

Council for Economic Planning Development. 1987. *Taiwan Statistical Data Book*.

Crawford, J.G. 1968. *Australian Trade Policy, 1942–1966*. Canberra: Australian National University Press.

――― and Saburo Okita. 1976. *Australia, Japan and Western Pacific Economic Relations*. A report to the Governments of Australia and Japan. Canberra: Australian Government Publishing Service.

Crawford, J.G. and G. Seow, eds. 1981. *Pacific Economic Cooperation: Suggestions for Action*. Malaysia: Heinemann Asia, for the Pacific Community Seminar.

Drysdale, Peter. 1969. "Japan, Australia, and New Zealand: The Prospect for Western Pacific Economic Integration". *Economic Record* 45, no.111.

———. 1970. "A Pacific Free Trade Area: An Australian View". In Kiyoshi Kojima, ed. *Papers and Proceedings of the Pacific Trade and Development Conference*. Tokyo: Japan Economic Research Centre.

———. 1984. "Pacific Trade and Development Conference: A Brief History". Pacific Economic Papers no.112. Canberra: Australia-Japan Research Centre, Australian National University.

———. 1988. *International Economic Pluralism: Economic Policy in East Asia and the Pacific*. New York: Columbia University Press/ Sydney: Allen & Unwin.

——— and R.G. Garnaut. 1982. "Trade Intensities and the Analysis of Bilateral Trade Flows in a Many-Country World". *Hitotsubashi Journal of Economics* 22, no.2 (February).

——— and R.G. Garnaut. 1989. "A Pacific Free Trade Area?" In Jeffery J. Schott, ed. *More Free Trade Areas?: Free Trade Areas and U.S. Trade Policy*. Washington, D.C.: Institute for International Economics.

——— and R.G. Garnaut. 1993. "The Pacific: An Application of a General Theory of Economic Integration". In C. Fred Bergsten and Marcus Nolan, eds. *Pacific Dynamism and the International Economic System*. Washington, D.C.: Institute of International Economics.

——— and Hugh Patrick. 1979. *An Asian-Pacific Regional Economic Organisation: An Exploratory Concept Paper*. Committee on Foreign Relations, United States Senate (Congressional Research Service), Washington, D.C.

Dunn, Lydia. 1983. *In the Kingdom of the Blind: A Report on Protectionism and the Asian-Pacific Region*. Special Report no.3. London: Trade Policy Research Centre.

Eagleburger, L. 1992. Statement on APEC Senior Officials Meeting, Washington, D.C.

Elek, A. 1992*a*. "Pacific Economic Co-operation: Policy Choices for the 1990s". *Asian-Pacific Economic Literature* 6, no.1 (May).

———. 1992*b*. "Trade Policy Options for the Asia-Pacific Region in the 1990s: the Potential of Open Regionalism". *American Economic Review* 82, no.2.

———. 1992*c*. "Regionalism in the World Economy: Implications for AFTA and ASEAN Trade Policy". Paper presented to the 17th Conference of the Federation of ASEAN Economic Associations, Surabaya.

Eminent Persons Group (EPG). 1993. *A Vision for APEC: Towards An Asia-Pacific Economic Community*. Singapore.

———. 1994. *Achieving the APEC Vision: Free and Open Trade in the Asia-Pacific*. Singapore.

Evans, Gareth. 1989. Chairman's Summary, APEC I. Canberra.

Findlay, Christopher and Ross Garnaut, eds. 1986. *The Political Economy of Manufacturing Protection: Experiences of ASEAN and Australia*. Sydney: Allen & Unwin.

Finlayson, Jock and Mark Zacher. 1981. "The GATT and the Regulation of Trade Barriers: Regional Dynamics and Functions". *International Organisation* 35, no.4.

Frankel, J.A. 1993. "Is Japan creating a yen block to East Asia and the Pacific". In Jeffrey A. Frankel and M. Kahler, eds. *Regionalism and Rivalry: Japan and the United States in Pacific Asia*. Chicago: University of Chicago Press.

Fynmore, R. and H. Hill. 1992. "Overview". *Australia's Business Challenge: Southeast Asia in the 1990s*. Canberra: AGPS.

Garnaut, Ross. 1972. "Australian Trade with Southeast Asia: A Study of Resistances to Bilateral Trade Flows". Doctoral dissertation, Australian National University, Canberra.

———, ed. 1980. *ASEAN in a Changing Pacific and World Economy*. Canberra: The Australian National University Press.

———. 1981. "Australian Trade Policy and Western Pacific Economic Growth", *Economic Papers*. Reprinted in part in J.G. Crawford and G. Seow, eds. *Pacific Economic Cooperation: Suggestions for Action*. Malaysia: Heinemann Asia, for the Pacific Community Seminar.

Garnaut, Ross. 1989. *Australia and the Northeast Asian Ascendancy*. Canberra: Australian Government Publishing Service.

———. 1991*a*. "Expanded Thoughts on Australia and the Northeast Asian Ascendancy". In J. Richardson, ed. *Northeast Asian Challenge: Debating the Garnaut Report*. Canberra Studies in World Affairs no.27. Department of International Relations, Australian National University.

———. 1991*b*. "The Market and the State in Economic Development: Applications to the International System". *Singapore Economic Review* XXXVI, no.2 (October).

———. 1996. "Economic Reform in India and China: An Essay in Honor of Heinz Wolfgang Arndt". *Journal of Asian Economics* 7, no.1: 29–47.

——— and Kym Anderson. 1980. "ASEAN Export Specialisation and the Evolution of Comparative Advantage in the Western Pacific Region". In Ross Garnaut, ed. *ASEAN in a Changing Pacific and World Economy*. Canberra: Australian National University Press.

——— and Peter Drysdale, eds. 1994. *Asia-Pacific Regionalism: Readings in International Economic Relations*. Sydney: HarperCollins Educational.

——— and Yiping Huang. 1994. "How Rich is China: More Evidence". Australia-Japan Research Centre, Australian National University.

——— and Guonan Ma. 1993. "How Rich is China: Evidence from the Food Economy". *Australian Journal of Chinese Affairs*, no.30, pp.121–48.

General Agreement on Tariffs and Trade. 1980. *Tariff Escalation*. Note by the Secretariat prepared for the Committee on Trade and Development, Forty-first Session.

Grossman, Gene M. and J. David Richardson. 1985. "Strategic Trade Policy: A Survey of Issues and Early Analysis". Special Papers in International Economics, 15. Princeton University.

Hathaway, Dale E. 1987. *Agriculture and the GATT: Rewriting the Rules*. Washington, D.C.: Institute for International Economics.

Hawke, Bob. 1983. Speech to Australia-Thai Chamber of Commerce. Bangkok.

———. 1989*a*. "Regional Co-operation, Challenges for Korea and Australia". Speech, Seoul.

———. 1989*b*. "Opening Statement". APEC I, Canberra.

Hay, Keith J. and B. Andrei Sulzenko. 1982. "US Trade Policy and 'Reciprocity'". *Journal of World Trade Law*. 16.

Hock, Lee Kiong. 1986. "Malaysia: The Structure and Causes of Manufacturing Sector Protection". In Christopher Findlay and Ross Garnaut, eds. *The Political Economy of Manufacturing Protection: Experiences of ASEAN and Australia*. Sydney: Allen & Unwin.

Hufbauer, Gary Clyde and Howard F. Rosen. 1986. *Trade Policy for Troubled Industries*. Washington, D.C.: Institute for International Economics.

International Economics, Essays in. Montreal: Institute for Research on Public Policy.

International Monetary Fund. 1988. *Direction of Trade*. Washington, D.C.: IMF.

Itoh, Motoshige. 1988. "Organisational Transactions and Japanese-Style Business Relations". Paper presented at a public seminar at the Australia-Japan Research Centre, Australian National University, Canberra, 5 September.

Johnson, H.G. 1976. *Trade Negotiations and the New International Monetary System*. Geneva: Graduate Institute of Studies/London: Trade Policy Research Centre.

———. 1968. *The Wicksell Lectures*. Stockholm.

Keating, Paul. 1988. *Economic Statement*. Canberra: Australian Government Publishing Service.

———. 1993. "Australia, Trade and Asia: The Quiet Revolution in the Australian Economy". *The Sydney Papers* (special Conference Edition) 5, no.2 (Autumn): 1–9.

Keating, Paul. 1994. Answer to Question on APEC from the Leader of the Opposition, Australian Commonwealth Parliamentary Debates, Vol. H. Of R. 198, p.3722.

Keohane, Robert O. 1986. "Reciprocity in International Relations". *International Organisation* 40, no.1.

————— and Joseph Nye. 1977. *Power and Interdependence: World Politics in Transition*. Boston: Little, Brown & Company.

Kojima, Kiyoshi. 1971. *Japan and a Pacific Free Trade Area*. London: Macmillan.

—————. 1977. *Japan and a New World Economic Order*. Tokyo: Tuttle and Co.

————— and Hiroshi Kurimoto. 1966. "A Pacific Economic Community and Asian Developing Countries". In *Measures for Trade Expansion of Developing Countries*. Tokyo: Japan Economic Research Center. Also published in *Hitotsubashi Journal of Economics* 7, no.1 (1966): 17–37.

Krasner, Stephen D. 1986. "Trade Conflicts and Common Defence: The United States and Japan". *Political Science Quarterly* 101, no.5.

Krause, L.B. 1992. "Trading and Investment Patterns Around the Pacific: Implications for the U.S. Economy". Paper to 40th Annual Economic Outlook Conference, University of Michigan.

————— and M. Sundberg. 1991. "The Pacific and the World Economy: Inter-relations". In M. Ariff, ed. *The Pacific Economy: Growth and External Stability*. Presented to the 18th Pacific Trade and Development Conference. Kuala Lumpur: Allen and Unwin.

Krueger, A.O. 1980. "Regional and Global Approaches to Trade and Development Strategy". In R. Garnaut, ed. *ASEAN in a Changing Pacific and World Economy*. Canberra: Australian National University Press.

Krugman, Paul. 1991. "The Move to Free Trade Zones". *Federal Reserve Bank of Kansas Review*. December.

—————. 1992. "Regionalism vs. Multilateralism: Analytical Notes". Paper presented at the World Bank-CPER Conference on Regional Integration, Washington, D.C., 2–3 April.

Lawrence, Robert Z. 1987. "Imports in Japan: Closed Markets or Minds?" *Brookings Papers on Economic Activity* 1.

Lee, Tsao Yuan, ed. 1991. *Growth Triangle: The Johor-Singapore-Riau Experience*. Singapore: Institute of Southeast Asian Studies.

Lipsey, R.G. 1960. "The Theory of Customs Unions: A General Survey". *The Economic Journal* 70.

MacMillan, J. 1990. "Game Theory and International Trade Negotiations". Canberra: Australian National University Seminar.

Milner, H. 1991. "A Three Block Trading System". IPSA Conference, July, Buenos Aires.

Pangestu, Mari and Boediono. 1986. "Indonesia: The Structure and Causes of Manufacturing Sector Protection". In Christopher Findlay and Ross Garnaut, eds. *The Political Economy of Manufacturing Protection: Experiences of ASEAN and Australia*. Sydney: Allen & Unwin.

Patrick, Hugh. 1987. "The Management of the United States-Japan Trade Relationships and its Implications for Pacific Basin Economies". Mimeo. Background paper for the Project on the Impact of Japan-US Economic Relations on Other Pacific Basin Nations. US National Committee for Pacific Economic Cooperation.

PECC (Pacific Economic Co-operation Council). 1992. "Accompanying Statement and San Francisco Declaration". San Francisco, 23–25 September. Reprinted in *ASEAN Economic Bulletin* 9, no.2 (November).

Riskin, C. 1996. "Rural Poverty in Post-Reform China". In Ross Garnaut, Guo Shutian and Ma Guonan, eds. *The Third Revolution in the Chinese Countryside*. Cambridge: Cambridge University Press.

Ruggiero, Renato. 1996. "Implications for Trade in a Borderless World". Speech of the Director-General of the World Trade Organisation to the World Trade Congress, Singapore.

Saxonhouse, Gary R. and Robert M. Stern. 1988. "An Analytical Survey of Formal and Informal Barriers to International Trade and Investment in the United States, Canada and Japan". University of Michigan Research Seminar on International Economics, Discussion Paper no. 215.

Snape, Richard. 1984. "Australia's Relations with GATT". *Economic Record* 60, no.168.

———. 1988. "Is Non-discrimination Dead?" *The World Economy* 11, no.1.

Soesastro, Hadi. 1983. "Institutional Aspects of Pacific Economic Cooperation". In Hadi Soesastro and Sung-Joo Han, eds. *Pacific Economic Cooperation: The Next Phase*. Jakarta: Centre for Strategic and International Studies. (Prepared originally as a report for ESCAP, Report on ASEAN and Pacific Economic Cooperation, Bangkok, June 1982, titled "Institutional Aspects of ASEAN-Pacific Economic Cooperation".)

Stoeckel, Andy and Sandy Cuthbertson. 1987. *Successful Strategies for Australian Trade*. Canberra: Centre for International Economics.

Summers, Robert and Alan Heston. 1984. "Improved International Comparison of Real Product and Its Composition: 1950–1980". *Review of Income and Wealth* (June).

Summers, Lawrence H. 1991. "Regionalism and the World Trading System". Paper presented at the Jackson Hole Conference on Free Trade Areas, Federal Reserve Bank of Kansas City, August.

Sung, Yun-Wing. 1992. "The Economic Integration of Hong Kong, Taiwan and South Korea with the Mainland of China". In Ross Garnaut and Liu Guoguang, eds. *Economic Reform and Internationalisation: China and the Pacific Region*. Sydney: Allan and Unwin.

Takeuchi, Kenji. 1988. "Does Japan Import Less Than It Should?". *Working Papers*, International Economics Development, World Bank.

Tan, Norma A. 1986. "The Philippines: The Structure and Causes of Manufacturing Sector Protection". In Christopher Findlay and Ross Garnaut, eds. *The Political Economy of Manufacturing Protection: Experiences of ASEAN and Australia*. Sydney: Allen & Unwin.

United Nations (various issues). *Monthly Bulletin of Statistics*. New York: United Nations Organisation.

Vanek, J. 1965. *General Equilibrium of International Discrimination: the Case of Customs Unions*. Cambridge, Massachusetts: Harvard University Press.

Vernon, R. 1966. "International Investment and International trade in the Produce Cycle". *Quarterly Journal of Economics* 79 (May).

Wonnacott, A.J. 1984. "Aggressive US Reciprocity Evaluated with a New Analytical Approach to Trade Conflicts". *Essays in International Economics*. Montreal: Institute for Research on Public Policy.

World Bank. 1987. *World Tables*. Washington, D.C.: World Bank.

Yamazawa, I. 1992. "On Pacific Economic Integration". *Economic Journal* 105, no. 415.

INDEX

208

About the Author

Ross Garnaut is Professor of Economics in the Research School of Pacific and Asian Studies at the Australian National University. He has been a central figure in the discussion of Asia-Pacific economic co-operation since the 1970s. His research interests are focused on economic development and international economic relations in East Asia and the Pacific. Recent books include *The Third Revolution in the Chinese Countryside* (Cambridge University Press, 1996) and, with Peter Drysdale, *Asia Pacific Regionalism: Readings in International Economic Relations* (Harper Educational, 1994)